IGCSE Mathematics

module 3

University of Cambridge Local Examinations Syndicate

Reviewed by **John Pitts**, Principal Examiner and Moderator for HIGCSE Mathematics

Edited by **Carin Abramovitz**

PUBLISHED BY THE PRESS SYNDICATE OF THE UNIVERSITY OF CAMBRIDGE
The Pitt Building, Trumpington Street, Cambridge CB2 1RP, United Kingdom

CAMBRIDGE UNIVERSITY PRESS
The Edinburgh Building, Cambridge CB2 2RU, UK http://www.cup.cam.ac.uk
40 West 20th Street, New York, NY 10011-4211, USA http://www.cup.org
10 Stamford Road, Oakleigh, Melbourne 3166, Australia
Dock House, Victoria and Alfred Waterfront, Cape Town 8001, South Africa

© University of Cambridge Local Examinations Syndicate 1998

This book is in copyright. Subject to statutory exception
and to the provisions of relevant collective licensing agreements,
no reproduction of any part may take place without
the written permission of Cambridge University Press.

First published 1998
Fourth printing 2002

Printed by Creda Communications, Cape Town

Typeface New Century Schoolbook 11.5/14 pt

A catalogue record for this book is available from the British Library

ISBN 0 521 62517 3 paperback

Acknowledgements
We would like to acknowledge the contribution made to these materials by the writers and
editors of the Namibian College of Open Learning (NAMCOL).

Illustrations by André Plant.

Contents

Introduction   iv

Unit 1   Graphs in Practical Situations   1
- A   Cartesian coordinates in two dimensions   2
- B   Interpreting and using graphs - part 1   4
- C   Interpreting and using graphs - part 2   15

Unit 2   Drawing and Using Algebraic Graphs   29
- A   Straight line graphs   29
- B   Some curved graphs   44
- C   Using graphs to solve equations   52

Unit 3   Other Algebraic Graphs   63
- A   Cubic curves   63
- B   Other curves   69
- C   The gradient of a curve   74

Unit 4   Function Notation and Linear Programming   83
- A   Functions   83
- B   Inequalities and regions in a plane   90
- C   Linear Programming   99

Solutions   113

Index   127

Introduction

Welcome to Module 3 of IGCSE Mathematics! This is the **third module** in a course of six modules designed to help you prepare for the International General Certificate of Secondary Education (IGCSE) Mathematics examinations. Before starting this module, you should have completed Module 2. If you are studying through a distance-education college, you should also have completed the **end-of-module assignment** for Module 2. The diagram below shows how this module fits into the IGCSE Mathematics course as a whole.

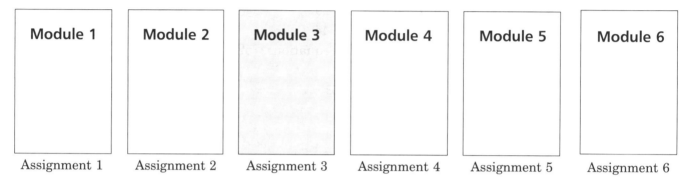

Like the previous module, this module should help you develop your mathematical knowledge and skills in particular areas. If you need help while you are studying this module, contact a **tutor** at your college or school. If you need more information on writing the examination, planning your studies, or how to use the different features of the modules, refer back to the **Introduction** at the beginning of Module 1.

Some study tips for Maths

- As you work through the course, it is very important that you use a **pen or pencil and exercise book**, and *work through the examples yourself* in your exercise book as you go along. Maths is not about reading, but about doing and understanding!
- Do feel free to write in pencil in this book – fill in steps that are left out and make your own notes in the margin.
- *Don't expect to understand everything the first time you read it.* If you come across something difficult, it may help if you read on – but make sure you come back later and go over it again until you understand it.
- You will need a **calculator** for doing mathematical calculations and a **dictionary** may be useful for looking up unfamiliar words.

Remember

- In the examination you will be required to give decimal approximations correct to **three significant figures** (unless otherwise indicated), e.g. 14.2 or 1 420 000 or 0.00142.
- Angles should be given to **one decimal place**, e.g. 43.5°. Try to get into the habit of answering in this way when you do the exercises.

The **table** below may be useful for you to keep track of where you are in your studies. Tick each block as you complete the work. Try to fit in study time whenever you can – if you have half an hour free in the evening, spend that time studying. Every half hour counts! You can study a **section**, and then have a break before going on to the next section. If you find your concentration slipping, have a break and start again when your mind is fresh. Try to plan regular times in your week for study, and try to find a quiet place with a desk and a good light to work by. Good luck with this module!

IGCSE MATHEMATICS MODULE 3

Unit no.	Unit title	Unit studied	'Check your progress' completed	Revised for exam
1	Graphs in Practical Situations			
2	Drawing and Using Algebraic Graphs			
3	Other Algebraic Graphs			
4	Function Notation and Linear Programming			

Unit 1
Graphs in Practical Situations

Until the 12th century, it was mostly the great Hindu and Muslim mathematicians who provided the world with mathematical techniques. In algebra, their work was concentrated on the solution of various types of equations.

Algebra and geometry were treated as separate subjects. But in the 12th century the great Persian mathematician Omar Khayyam showed that accurate drawings of curves could be used to solve cubic equations (for example, $x^3 = x^2 + 2x - 1$). During the 16th century, three developments set the scene for a rapid expansion in mathematics:

- the invention of accurate mechanical clocks stimulated an interest in the mathematics of time and quantities which change with time
- the increasing use of artillery in warfare stimulated an interest in the mathematics of projectiles
- the need to discover ways to navigate long distances out of sight of land stimulated an interest in the mathematics of map making.

In the 17th century, mathematicians began to apply algebra to the study of geometry and to use geometry to solve problems in algebra. Credit for the development is given to the French mathematicians René Descartes and Blaise Pascal. The branch of mathematics which deals with the interaction of algebra and geometry is called **coordinate geometry** or **cartesian geometry** (in honour of Descartes).

> You say **coordinate** in two words, like this: **co ordinate**.

In cartesian geometry you show the relationship between two variables by plotting points and drawing graphs on a grid. You'll study the method in this module. First you'll learn how to draw a graph and then I'll show you how to interpret information from graphs.

This unit is divided into three sections:

Section	Title	Time
A	Cartesian coordinates in two dimensions	1 hour
B	Interpreting and using graphs – part 1	$4\frac{1}{2}$ hours
C	Interpreting and using graphs – part 2	5 hours

By the end of this unit, you should be able to:

- understand and use cartesian coordinates in two dimensions
- interpret graphs representing real-life situations
- draw graphs from given data
- calculate speed from a linear distance–time graph
- calculate acceleration from a linear speed–time graph
- calculate distance from a linear speed–time graph.

A Cartesian coordinates in two dimensions

The position of a ship at sea can be reported in different ways. You could give:
- its longitude and latitude
- its distance and bearing from a fixed point (for example, a lighthouse)
- its distance east and its distance north of a fixed point.

Notice that, in each case, *two* quantities are needed to fix the ship's position. This is because the ship is moving on the earth so it has two degrees of freedom – for example, it can move east/west and north/south independently.

In developing cartesian geometry, the French mathematician René Descartes made use of the fact that the position of a point on a flat surface can be specified by giving two numbers. The two numbers he used correspond to the distances east and north mentioned above for the ship.

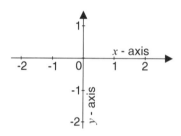

Descartes began with two number lines at right angles to each other, as shown in the diagram.

The **horizontal** line is called the x-axis.

The **vertical** line is called the y-axis. These two axes are the basis of the cartesian coordinate system.

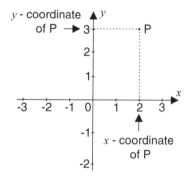

The position of any point is given as an **ordered pair** of numbers, written in brackets. For example, P is the point (2,3). The first number is read off the x-axis (as shown in the diagram) and is called the x-coordinate of the point. The second number is read off the y-axis. It is called the y-coordinate of the point.

Note that the order is important. The x-coordinate is *always* first and the y-coordinate is *always* second. (2,3) and (3,2) are two different points. That's why we say that (2,3) is an **ordered** pair.

The point where the x-axis and the y-axis cross is called the **origin** of the coordinate system. The origin is usually given the letter O. Its coordinates are (0, 0).

Examples

1.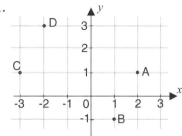

   In the diagram:
   point A has coordinates (2, 1)
   point B has coordinates (1, −1)
   point C has coordinates (−3, 1)
   point D has coordinates (−2, 3)

   Notice that if you join A, B, C, D they are the corners of a rectangle.

2.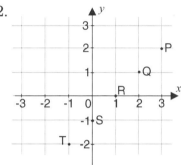

   In the diagram:
   point P has coordinates (3, 2)
   point Q has coordinates (2, 1)
   point R has coordinates (1, 0)
   point S has coordinates (0, −1)
   point T has coordinates (−1, −2)

   Notice that P, Q, R, S, T are in a straight line.

3.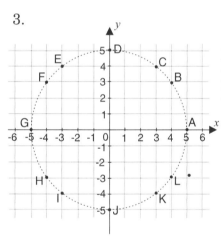

   In the diagram, the points A (5, 0), B (4, 3), C (3, 4), D (0, 5), E (−3, 4), F (−4, 3), G (−5, 0), H (−4, −3), I (−3, −4), J (0, −5), K (3, −4), L (4, −3) are plotted.

   Notice that (4, 3) and (3, 4) are different points. So are (−3, 4) and (4, −3). Notice also that the twelve points all lie on a circle whose centre is at the origin and whose radius is 5 units.

Answer the following questions to see whether you have a good understanding of how to work with coordinates. Make sure that you do before you continue with the work in this module.

EXERCISE 1

1.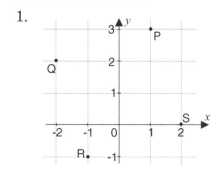

   a) Write down the coordinates of the points P, Q, R, S shown in the diagram.
   b) If the lines PQ, QR, RS, SP are drawn, what shape is formed?

2. 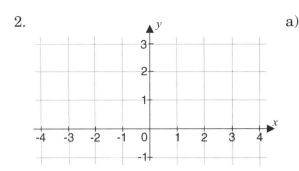   a) On the diagram plot the following:

   point A with coordinates (4, 3),
   point B with coordinates (2, 2),
   point C with coordinates (−4, −1).

   b) The points A, B, C are in a straight line. Find the coordinates of the points where this straight line crosses the x- and y-axes.

3. 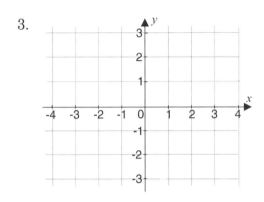   a) On the diagram, plot the following:

   point H with coordinates (3, 1),
   point I with coordinates (−1, 3),
   point J with coordinates (−3, 0),
   point K with coordinates (3, −3).

   b) What do you notice about the lines IH and JK?
   c) If the lines HI, IJ, JK, KH are drawn, what shape is formed?

Check your answers at the end of this module.

B Interpreting and using graphs – part 1

You've seen graphs used in newspapers and on television. They're also used a lot in business reports and government publications. Most people find graphs easier to understand than the columns of figures which were used to obtain the graphs.

In Section A you saw that any point on a plane (a flat surface) can be represented by two coordinates, the x-coordinate and the y-coordinate. This means that we can use a cartesian graph to illustrate a mathematical relationship between two quantities, the x-quantity and the y-quantity.

Once a graph has been drawn, further information can be found from it, usually by reading off values on the horizontal axis (the x-axis) or the vertical axis (the y-axis). Most of the errors learners make in graph work are connected with the scales on the axes. Remember that:

- when drawing a graph, make sure that the spaces between the numbers on an axis are equal
- before reading off values from a graph, work out what each small square represents on each of the axes.

Example 1 and solution

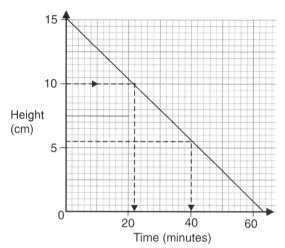

This graph shows the change in height of a candle as it burns. Notice that both the axes are labelled clearly. The vertical axis shows the height of the candle measured in centimetres. The horizontal axis represents the time in minutes that the candle burns. Without labels on the axes the graph would have no meaning.

On the horizontal (time) axis, 10 small squares represent 20 minutes, so each small square represents 2 minutes. On the vertical (height) axis, 10 small squares represent 5 cm, so each small square represents 0.5 cm.

Here is some of the information which can be obtained from the graph:

a) The unlit candle was 15 cm high.
b) It takes 21 minutes for the candle to burn down to a height of 10 cm. (Note the lines drawn on the graph.)
c) After 40 minutes, the height of the candle is 5.5 cm.
d) It takes 63 minutes for the candle to burn out completely.

Example 2

The strength of concrete increases according to the number of days that it has been laid. The graph shows how this increase progresses.

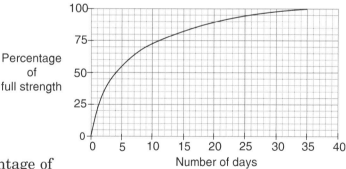

a) What percentage of the full strength does the concrete have after 3 weeks?
b) How many days does the concrete take to reach half strength?
c) How many days does it take for the strength to increase from 70% to 80%?

Solution

a) Each small square on the horizontal axis represents 1 day. 3 weeks = 21 days. A line drawn vertically from 21 days on the horizontal axis meets the curve 3 small squares above 75%. Each small square on the vertical axis represents 5%. So, after 3 weeks the concrete is 90% of the full strength.

b) 'Half strength' means the concrete is 50% of full strength. A line drawn horizontally from 50% on the vertical axis meets the curve 4 small squares to the right of the vertical axis. Each small square on the horizontal axis represents 1 day. So, it takes 4 days for the concrete to reach half strength.

c) On the vertical axis, 70% is one small square below 75% and 80% is one small square above 75%. Drawing the appropriate horizontal lines on the graph, we see the strength is 70% after 9 days and it is 80% after $13\frac{1}{2}$ days. So it takes $4\frac{1}{2}$ days for the strength to increase from 70% to 80%.

Example 3

The graph shows the concentration of vaccine in the blood for 7 hours after a person has been vaccinated.

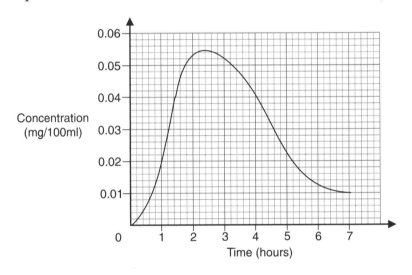

a) After what times is the concentration of vaccine 0.02 mg/100 ml?

b) What is the concentration of vaccine in the blood after 5 hours? Give your answer to 3 decimal places.

Solution

Each small square on the horizontal axis represents $\frac{1}{5}$ hour (or 12 minutes). Each small square on the vertical axis represents $\frac{0.01}{5}$ (or 0.002) mg/100 ml.

0.002 mg/100 ml means 0.002 milligrams of vaccine in every 100 millilitres of blood.

a) Starting at 0.02 on the vertical axis, draw a horizontal line. This meets the curve at two points. Draw a vertical line through each of these points to meet the horizontal axis and read off the *x*-coordinates – they are 1 and 5.2.
The times at which the concentration of vaccine is 0.02 mg/100 ml are 1 hour and 5.2 hours.
That is 1 hour and 5 hours 12 minutes.

b) Starting at 5 on the horizontal axis, draw a vertical line. This meets the curve at a point 1 small square above the level of the mark 0.02 on the vertical axis.

It follows that the concentration of vaccine in the blood after 5 hours is (0.02 + 1 × 0.002) mg/100ml.

That is 0.022 mg/100 ml to 3 decimal places.

Example 4

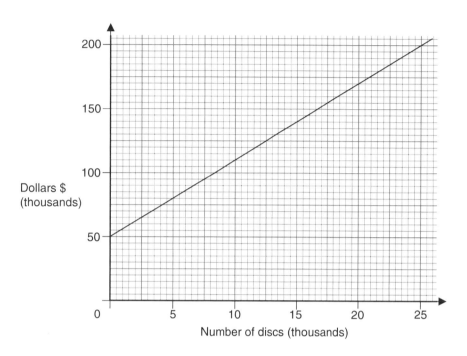

The graph shows the total cost of making compact discs.

a) The total cost is the sum of two parts. There is a fixed amount, plus a cost for making each disc.
    (i) What is the fixed amount?
    (ii) What is the cost for making each disc?
b) Discs are sold for $10 each.
    (i) Complete this table.

Number of discs sold (thousands)	0	5	10	15	20
Amount received (thousands of $)	0	50	100		

    (ii) Plot these points on the grid, and join them with a straight line.
c) How many discs must be made and sold before there is a profit?
d) If 18 000 discs are made and sold, how much profit is made?

Solution

a) (i) The fixed amount is the money spent before any discs can be made. From the graph, when the number of discs = 0, the cost = 50 thousand dollars. Thus, the fixed amount = $50 000.

(ii) From the graph, when the number of discs = 25 thousand, the total cost = $ 200 000.
$50 000 is the fixed amount, so the additional cost for making 25 thousand discs is $ 150 000.
So the cost for making each disc = $\frac{150\ 000}{25\ 000}$ = $ 6.

b) (i)

Number of discs sold (thousands)	0	5	10	15	20
Amount received (thousands of $)	0	50	100	150	200

(iii) The graph is shown below.

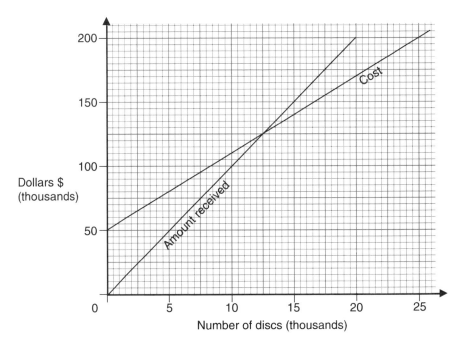

c) The two lines cross at the point with coordinates (12.5, 125). This means that when 12.5 thousand discs are made and sold, the amount received is equal to the total cost of making the discs.

So 12 500 discs must be made and sold before there is any profit.

d) On the horizontal axis, 18 (thousand) is 6 small squares to the right of 15 (thousand).

From the graph, the total cost of making the discs = $ 158 000 and the amount received by selling the discs = $ 180 000.

So the profit made = $ 180 000 − $ 158 000
= $ 22 000.

Conversion graphs You often have to change measurements on one scale into measurements on another scale. For example, you may want to change a distance measured in miles into kilometres, or the cost of a book given in Deutschmarks to rands. A graph is a useful way of doing this conversion.

A conversion graph is usually a straight line, so you need to plot only two points and join them (although plotting a third point is a useful check). Many conversion graphs go through the origin (0, 0), in which case the two variables are *directly proportional*.

Distance in miles is directly proportional to distance in kilometres. Cost in Deutschmarks is directly proportional to cost in rands. Although the graph for converting temperatures in °F to °C is a straight line, it does not pass through the origin because 0 °F is not the same as 0 °C.

Temperature in °F is *not* directly proportional to temperature in °C.

Example 1

Taking 5 miles to be the same as 8 kilometres, draw a graph to convert miles into kilometres.

Solution

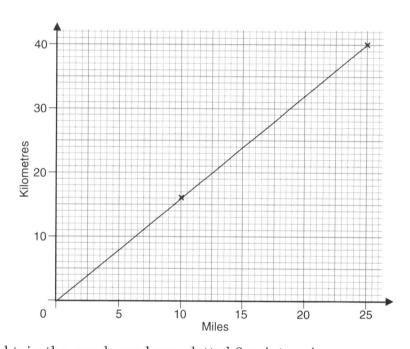

To obtain the graph, we have plotted 3 points using:

   0 miles = 0 kilometres
 10 miles = 16 kilometres
 25 miles = 40 kilometres

On the horizontal axis, one small square represents 0.5 miles. On the vertical axis, one small square represents 1 kilometre.

Using the graph, we obtain results such as:
   20 kilometres = 12.5 miles
   27 kilometres = 17 miles
   20 miles = 32 kilometres
   12 miles = 19 kilometres

Example 2

The freezing point of water is 0 °C or 32 °F.
The boiling point of water is 100 °C or 212 °F.
Use this information to draw a conversion graph for temperatures.

Solution

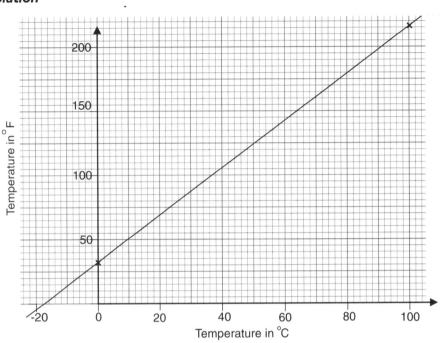

Here we have shown °C on the horizontal axis and °F on the vertical axis. It would not be incorrect to have them the other way round. (This applies to all conversion graphs.)

On the horizontal axis, one small square represents 2 °C. On the vertical axis, a small square represents 5 °F.

Using the graph, we obtain results such as
60 °C = 140 °F   16 °C = 60 °F
 0 °F = −18 °C   190 °F = 88 °C

Travel graphs

Graphs which show the connection between the distance of an object (measured along a fixed path from a fixed point) and the time are called **distance–time graphs** or **travel graphs**.

Example 1

Suppose you make a journey as follows:

- you walk for 4 minutes from your home to a bus stop 1 km away
- you wait for 2 minutes for a bus
- you travel 7 km in 10 minutes on the bus to reach your destination.

Draw a travel graph of your journey.

Solution

Here is the travel graph for your journey.

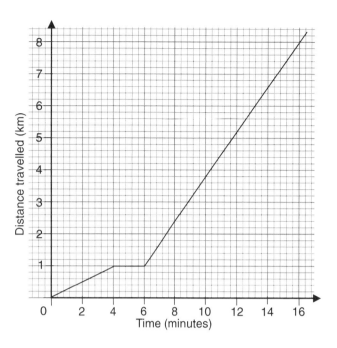

Notice that:

- the graph starts at the origin because, at the beginning, no time has elapsed and no distance has been travelled
- while you are waiting for the bus, the distance from home remains at 1 km although time moves on (the *horizontal* line indicated that you are not moving)
- the part of the graph for the bus journey is steeper than the part for the walk because the bus travels faster than you walk.

Example 2

Ken's school is 4 km away from his home and it takes him 40 minutes to walk to school. One morning, he sets off at 7 a.m. but after 15 minutes he realises that he has forgotten his football boots. He runs back home in 10 minutes. It takes him 3 minutes to find the boots and he then runs at the same speed to school. Draw a travel graph for Ken.

Solution

This is Ken's travel graph.

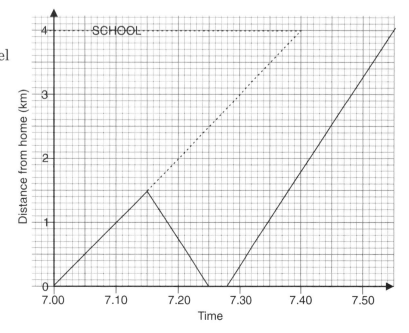

Notice that:
- if he had not forgotten his boots, Ken would have reached school at 7.40 a.m.
- Ken walked 1.5 km before he remembered his boots
- the graph goes downwards as Ken runs towards home
- the horizontal part of the graph corresponds to the 3 minutes Ken is at home
- running to school at the same speed means that Ken ran the first 1.5 km towards school in 10 minutes – the graph is then extended until it reaches the level of the 4 km mark on the vertical scale
- Ken reached school at 7.55 a.m.

You have now studied a variety of graphs and it is time for you to tackle some questions to test your understanding.

EXERCISE 2

1.
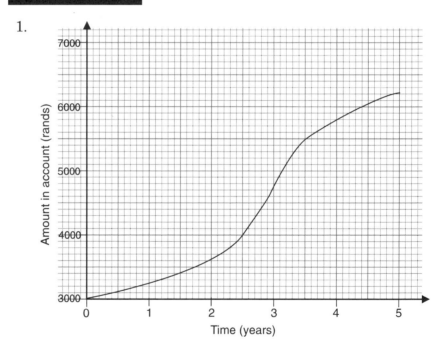

Moses invested R3000 in a special savings account. The interest rate was variable. The graph shows the amount in the account over the first 5 years.

a) What does one small square on the horizontal axis represent?
b) What does one small square on the vertical axis represent?
c) What was the amount in the account after 3 years?
d) How long did it take for the amount in the account to reach R5500?
e) How long did it take for the amount in the account to rise from R4000 to R6000?
f) After how long was the amount in the account rising most rapidly?

2. This is a conversion graph for kilograms and pounds.

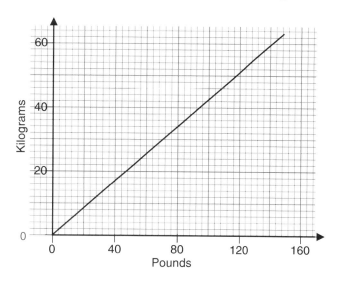

Use the graph to answer the questions below.

a) What does one small square on the horizontal axis represent?
b) What does one small square on the vertical axis represent?
c) Change 80 pounds to kilograms.
d) The minimum weight to qualify as an amateur lightweight boxer is 57 kg. What is this weight in pounds?
e) Which of the following conversions are incorrect? What should they be?
  (i) 30 kg = 66 pounds
 (ii) 18 pounds = 40 kg
(iii) 60 pounds = 37 kg
(iv) 20 pounds = 9 kg

3. Look at this grid:

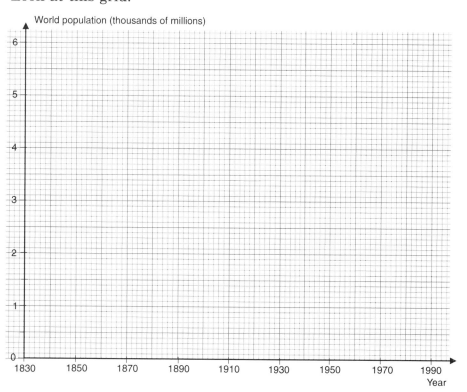

a) What does one small square represent:
   (i) on the year axis
   (ii) on the world population axis

b)
Year	1830	1890	1927	1960	1974	1987	1998
World population (thousands of millions)	1	1.5	2	3	4	5	6

Represent the information above by plotting points on the grid. Join up the seven points you have plotted with a smooth curve.

c) Use your graph to answer these questions.
   (i) In what year was the population of the world 2500 million?
   (ii) What was the population of the world in 1980?
   (iii) Find the increase in the world population between 1830 and 1850.
   (iv) Describe how the population of the world is changing.

4. This distance–time graph represents Monica's journey from home to a supermarket and back home again.

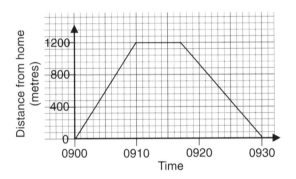

a) How far was Monica from home at 0906 hours?
b) How many minutes was Monica at the supermarket?
c) At what times was Monica 800 m from home?
d) On which part of the journey did Monica travel faster – going to the supermarket or returning home?

5. Omar left school at 1630. On his way home he stayed at his friend's house before going home on his bicycle. The travel graph shows this information.

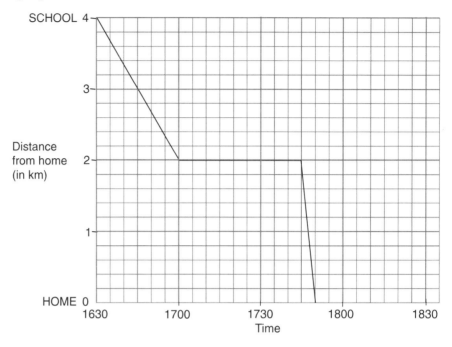

a) How long did he stay at his friend's house?
b) At what time did Omar arrive home?
c) Omar's brother left school at 1645 and walked home using the same route as Omar. He arrived home at the same time as Omar.
  (i) Show his journey accurately on the travel graph.
  (ii) At what time did he pass Omar's friend's house?

When you have tried all the questions in this exercise (and not before!), you should check your answers at the end of this module.

The remainder of the work in Section B is for learners following the EXTENDED syllabus. Learners following the CORE syllabus only, should now turn to the 'Summary' on page 24.

C Interpreting and using graphs – part 2

Representation of speed in a distance–time graph

Did you notice that we sometimes obtained information from a travel graph by considering the steepness of the graph?

- A straight line graph indicates a constant speed.
- The steeper the graph, the greater the speed.
- The graph sloping upwards and the graph sloping downwards represent movements in opposite directions.

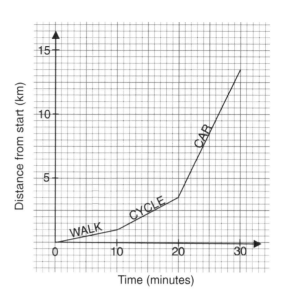

This distance–time graph is for a person who walks, cycles and then travels by car, for three equal periods of time. For each period, the speed is given by the formula:

$$\text{speed} = \frac{\text{distance travelled}}{\text{time taken}}$$

The greater the speed, the greater the distance travelled, and the steeper the graph.

We need to be more precise about what we mean by the 'steepness' of a line which is part of a graph.

In this diagram, the steepness of the line AB is measured by

$$\frac{\text{increase in } y\text{-coordinate}}{\text{increase in } x\text{-coordinate}}$$

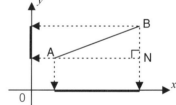

This is the same as $\frac{\text{NB (measured on the } y\text{-scale)}}{\text{AN (measured on the } x\text{-scale)}}$ and this is called the **gradient** of the line.

The gradient of a line can be positive, zero or negative. It is:
- positive if the line slopes upwards from left to right   ╱ '+' gradient
- zero if the line is horizontal   ──── 0 gradient
- negative if the line slopes downwards from left to right   ╲ '−' gradient

---

For a distance–time graph, a positive gradient indicates the object is moving in the direction of y increasing (that is 'distance' increasing), a zero gradient indicates that the object is not moving, and a negative gradient indicates that the object is moving in the direction of y decreasing (that is 'distance' decreasing).

For a distance–time graph,

$$\frac{\text{change in } y\text{-coordinate (distance)}}{\text{change in } x\text{-coordinate (time)}} = \frac{\text{distance travelled}}{\text{time taken}} = \text{speed}$$

and so the gradient gives us the speed of the object *and* its direction of motion. This is usually known as the **velocity** of the object. You should take particular note of this result:

> for a distance-time graph, gradient = velocity

Example 1 and solution

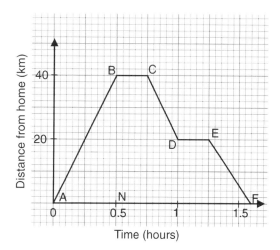

This travel graph represents a car journey. The horizontal sections BC and DE have zero gradient. They represent parts of the journey when the car's speed was zero – the car was not moving.

For the section AB, the gradient is positive.
Gradient $= \dfrac{\text{NB}}{\text{AN}} = \dfrac{40\,(\text{km})}{0.5\,(\text{hour})} = 80$

so the velocity was 80 km/h in the direction away from home.

For the section CD, the gradient is negative.
Gradient $= \dfrac{20 - 40\,(\text{km})}{0.25\,(\text{hour})} = -80$

so the velocity was 80 km/h in the direction towards home.

For the section EF, the gradient is negative.
Gradient $= \dfrac{0 - 20\,(\text{km})}{0.35\,(\text{hour})} = -57.1$

so the velocity was 57.1 km/h in the direction towards home.

Example 2

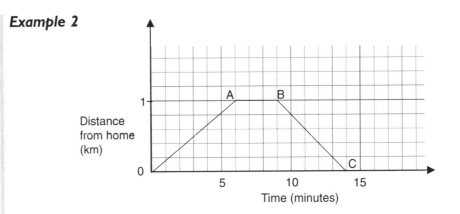

The travel graph above shows Hassan's daily run. He runs 1 km from home, rests, and then runs back home.

a) For how many minutes does he run before he takes a rest?
b) Calculate the speed, in kilometres per hour, at which he runs before he takes a rest.
c) For how many minutes does he rest?
d) Calculate his speed, in metres per minute, at which he runs back home.

Solution

a) The time in minutes is the *x*-coordinate of the point A.
Each small square on the horizontal axis represents 1 minute. So, the time Hassan runs before taking a rest is 6 minutes.

b) Hassan runs 1 km in 6 minutes.
1 hour = 60 minutes so Hassan's speed was 10 kilometres per hour.

c) The horizontal line from A to B represents the period when Hassan is resting. We deduce that Hassan rests for 3 minutes.

d) The *velocity* on the return journey is the gradient of the line BC on the graph. B has coordinates (9, 1) and C has coordinates (14, 0).

Gradient of BC $= \frac{0-1}{14-9} = -\frac{1}{5}$.

The minus sign indicates that Hassan is running towards home. The *speed* is $\frac{1}{5}$ kilometres per minute (taking into account the units of distance and time on the axes).

Thus, the speed is $\frac{1000}{5}$ metres per minute, that is 200 metres per minute.

> Notice that this is 12 kilometres per hour – Hassan's speed on the return journey is greater than his speed on the outward journey. This is represented on the graph by the fact that BC is steeper than OA.

The speed–time (or velocity–time) graph

The travel graphs we have considered so far have consisted of straight lines. This means that the speed of the object is constant for specified periods of time.

We now consider cases where the speed of the object is changing. We say that the object is **accelerating** if its speed is increasing and that it is **decelerating** if its speed is decreasing.

In this section, we will consider cases where the speed is increasing or decreasing at a steady rate over specified periods of time.

Example 1 and solution

This speed–time graph is for a train travelling between two stations.

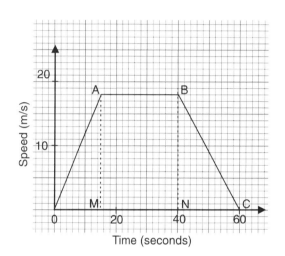

The train starts with zero speed. Its speed increases steadily, reaching 18 m/s in 15 seconds. The train then travels at a constant speed of 18 m/s for 25 seconds. It then slows down at a steady rate and comes to a stop. The whole journey between the stations took 60 seconds.

During the first part of the journey, the speed of the train increases by 18 m/s in 15 seconds. This is a rate of 1.2 m/s every second. This rate is the acceleration of the train and it would usually be written as 1.2 m/s^2. [metres per second becomes (m/s)/s which becomes m/s^2]

You will realise that $\frac{18 \text{ (m/s)}}{15 \text{ (seconds)}}$ is the gradient of the line representing the first part of the journey.

This is a particular example of the general result:

> for a speed–time graph, gradient = acceleration

During the last part of the train's journey, the speed decreases from 18 m/s to 0 m/s in 20 seconds. This is a rate of 0.9 m/s every second. This rate is the deceleration of the train and it is written as 0.9 m/s^2.

Notice that the gradient of the line representing the last part of the journey is $\frac{0 - 18 \text{ (m/s)}}{20 \text{ (seconds)}}$ which is -0.9. The negative sign corresponds to the fact that the train is decelerating.

Here's another important result concerning speed–time graphs. Consider the first part of the train's journey. The average speed over the 15 seconds is $\frac{1}{2}(0 + 18)$ m/s $= 9$ m/s. The distance travelled is $9 \times 15 = 135$ m.

[distance = speed × time]

(Notice that $\frac{1}{2}(18 \times 15) = 135$ is also the area of triangle OAM.)

For the middle part of the journey, the speed is 18 m/s for 25 seconds so the distance travelled is $18 \times 25 = 450$ m.
(Notice that (18×25) is also the area of rectangle AMNB.)

For the last part of the journey, the average speed over the 20 seconds is $\frac{1}{2}(18 + 0) = 9$ m/s. The distance travelled is $9 \times 20 = 180$ m.
(Notice that $\frac{1}{2}(18 \times 20)$ is also the area of triangle BNC.)

The total distance travelled by the train is $(135 + 450 + 180) = 765$ m and this is the same as (area OAM + area AMNB + area BNC) = area OABC.

This is a particular example of the important general result:

| for a speed–time graph, area under graph = distance travelled |

Example 2

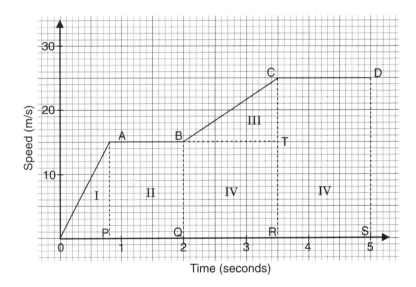

This speed–time graph represents the motion of a particle over a period of 5 seconds.
a) During which periods of time was the particle accelerating?
b) Calculate the particle's acceleration 3 seconds after the start.
c) Calculate the distance travelled by the particle in the 5 seconds.

Solution

a) The particle was accelerating in the period 0 to 0.8 seconds (section OA of the graph) and in the period 2 to 3.5 seconds (section BC).

b) The acceleration was constant in the period 2 to 3.5 seconds so the acceleration 3 seconds after the start $= \dfrac{25 - 15 \,(\text{m/s})}{3.5 - 2 \,(\text{seconds})} = \dfrac{10 \,(\text{m/s})}{1.5 \,(\text{s})} = 6\frac{2}{3}$ m/s². $\left[\text{acceleration} = \dfrac{\text{speed}}{\text{time}}\right]$

c) Distance travelled = area under graph
= area I + area II + area III + area IV + area V
= $\frac{1}{2}(0.8 \times 15) + (1.2 \times 15) + \frac{1}{2}(1.5 \times 10) + (1.5 \times 15) + (1.5 \times 25)$
= 6 + 18 + 7.5 + 22.5 + 37.5
= 91.5 m

> **Important note about units**
> When calculating acceleration and distance travelled from a speed–time graph, it is essential that the unit of speed on the vertical axis involves the same unit of time as on the horizontal axis.
> In both of the examples above, the speed unit was metres per second and the horizontal axis was graduated in seconds. These units are compatible.
> If the units of time are not the same, it is essential that the unit on one of the axes is converted into a compatible unit.

Example 3

The diagram is the distance–time graph of a short car journey. The greatest speed reached is 60 km/h. The acceleration in the first 2 minutes and the deceleration in the last 2 minutes are both constant.

a) Draw the speed–time graph of the journey.
b) Calculate the average speed, in kilometres per hour, for the journey.

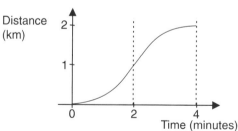

Solution

a) Since the acceleration and deceleration are both constant, the speed–time graph consists of straight lines. The greatest speed is 60 km/h so the speed–time graph is as shown in this diagram.

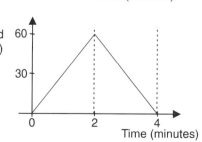

b) From the distance–time graph, the distance travelled in 4 minutes = 2 km.
So the average speed $= \dfrac{2 \text{ km}}{4 \text{ minutes}} = \dfrac{2 \text{ km} \times 15}{60 \text{ minutes}} = 30$ km/h.

> I multiplied 4 by 15 to get 60 minutes (1 hour) so I had to multiply the numerator by 15 as well

Example 4

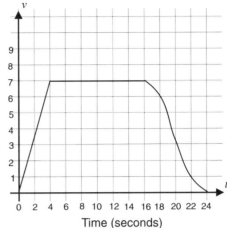

Speed (metres/second)
Time (seconds)

The diagram shows a speed–time graph for a bicycle journey.
a) Find the acceleration for the part of the journey:
    (i) during the first 4 seconds
    (ii) during the next 12 seconds
b) Find the distance travelled during the first 16 seconds.
c) Estimate the distance travelled during the last 8 seconds of the journey.

Solution

a) (i) The speed increases from 0 to 7 m/s in 4 seconds.
   Acceleration $= \frac{7 \text{ m/s}}{4 \text{ s}} = 1.75$ m/s^2.
   (ii) The graph is horizontal from 4 seconds to 16 seconds so the acceleration during this period is zero.

b) Distance travelled during the first 16 seconds
   = area under graph from time = 0 to time = 16
   = ($\frac{1}{2}(4 \times 7) + (12 \times 7)$) m = 98 m.

c) Distance travelled during last 8 seconds
   = area under graph from time = 16 to time = 24.

   This area has to be estimated by counting squares. There are 10 complete squares and the part squares add up to about $3\frac{1}{2}$ squares. A total of $13\frac{1}{2}$.

   Each square represents 1 m/s × 2 seconds, that is 2 m. So the distance travelled in the last 8 seconds
   = $13\frac{1}{2} \times 2$ m = 27 m.

You should now be able to answer the questions in the following exercise.

EXERCISE 3

1.

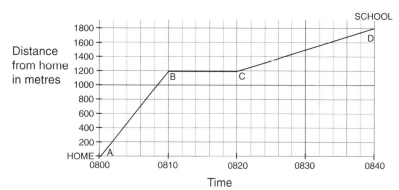

The distance–time graph above represents Ibrahim's journey from home to school one morning.

a) How far was Ibrahim from home at 0830 hours?
b) How fast, in m/s, was Ibrahim travelling during the first 10 minutes?
c) Describe the stage of Ibrahim's journey represented by the line BC.
d) How fast, in m/s, was Ibrahim travelling during the last 20 minutes?

2.

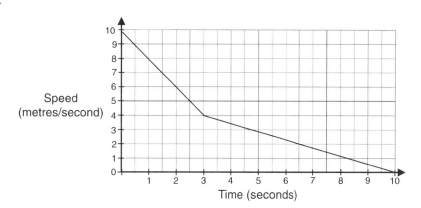

The graph shows the speed, in metres/second, of a car as it comes to rest from a speed of 10 m/s.

a) Calculate the rate at which the car is slowing down during the first 3 seconds.
b) Calculate the distance travelled during the 10 second period shown on the graph.
c) Calculate the average speed of the car for this 10 second period.

3.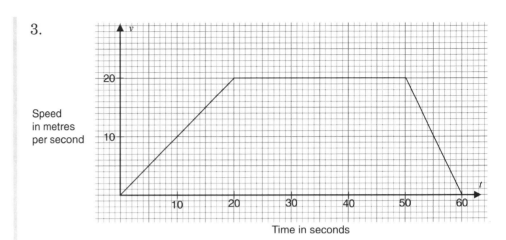

Time in seconds

The diagram above is the speed–time graph for a car journey.

a) Calculate the acceleration during the first 20 seconds of the journey.
b) Calculate the distance travelled in the last 10 seconds of the journey.
c) Calculate the average speed for the whole journey.

Summary

In this unit you learnt:
- to use x- and y-coordinates to plot points on the cartesian plane
- to interpret and draw graphs
- to work with distance–time graphs (travel graphs).

Students studying the EXTENDED syllabus should also remember that with a distance–time graph:
- a horizontal line means no distance is travelled
- positive and negative gradients indicate opposite directions
- a steeper gradient means a faster speed
- average speed $= \frac{\text{distance travelled}}{\text{time taken}}$.

With a speed–time graph:
- acceleration $= \frac{\text{speed}}{\text{time}}$
- distance travelled = area under graph.

In the next unit you'll learn about different kinds of algebraic graphs.

Check your progress

1. a) Write down the coordinates of the points P, Q, R which are marked on this grid.

   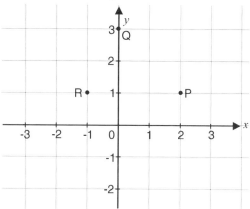

   b) The points P, Q, R together with another point S are the corners of a parallelogram (a four sided figure which has its opposite sides parallel). There are three possible positions for S. Mark them on the grid and write down their coordinates.

2. The graph shows the cost of repair work carried out by an electrician.

   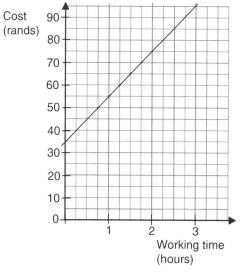

   a) What is the cost of work which takes $1\frac{3}{4}$ hours to complete?

   b) If the cost of work was R85, how long did the electrician take to do the work?

   c) The cost is made up of a fixed charge, p rands, together with a cost of q rands per hour.
   Find the value of p and the value of q.

3. The graph shows the changes which take place when a substance is heated.

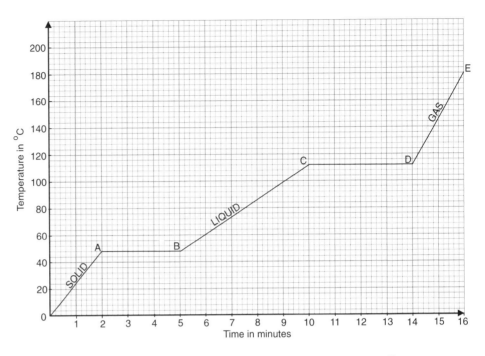

a) How many degrees are represented by one small square on the temperature axis?
b) Write down the temperature after 9 minutes.
c) After how many minutes was the temperature 130°C?
d) Calculate the average rate of increase in temperature over the whole 16 minute period.
e) In which state (solid, liquid or gas) is the temperature increasing most quickly? Explain how the graph helps to answer this.

4. A lorry driver who is delivering goods to North Africa finds that fuel is sold in US gallons. He usually buys fuel in litres.

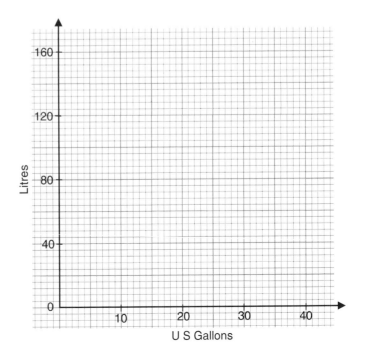

a) Taking 1 US gallon to be 3.8 litres, draw a conversion graph for US gallons and litres.
b) The driver knows the fuel tank will hold 90 litres. How many gallons is this?
c) The lorry will travel 5 km on a litre of fuel. How far will it travel on 1 gallon of fuel?

5. A swimming pool has a length of 25 m. Jasmine swims from one end to the other in 20 seconds. She rests for 10 seconds and then swims back to her starting point. It takes her 30 seconds to swim the second length.

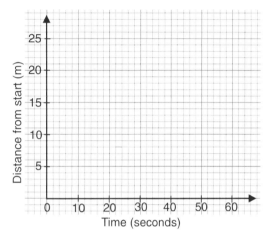

a) Draw a distance–time graph for Jasmine's swim.
b) How far was Jasmine from her starting point after 12 seconds?
c) How far was Jasmine from her finishing point after 54 seconds?

6.
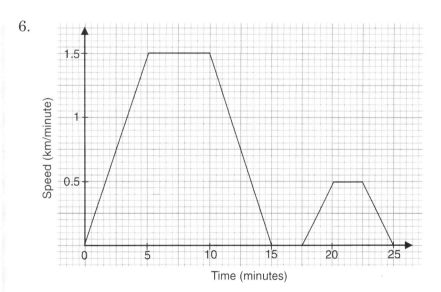

The speed–time graph above represents the journey of a train between two stations. The train slowed down and stopped after 15 minutes because of engineering work on the railway line.

a) Calculate the greatest speed, in km/h, which the train reached.
b) Calculate the deceleration of the train as it approached the place where there was engineering work.
c) Calculate the distance the train travelled in the first 15 minutes.
d) For how long was the train stopped, at the place where there was engineering work?
e) What was the speed of the train after 19 minutes?
f) Calculate the distance between the two stations.

Check your answers at the end of this module.

Unit 2
Drawing and Using Algebraic Graphs

You've looked at how graphs can be used to describe situations in real life. In this unit you'll learn about different kinds of graphs and some techniques for drawing them.

This unit is divided into three sections:

Section	Title	Time
A	Straight line graphs	4 hours
B	Some curved graphs	2 hours
C	Using graphs to solve equations	2 hours

By the end of this unit, you should be able to:
- construct tables of values for $y = mx + c$ and draw straight line graphs
- find the gradient of a straight line graph
- interpret m and c in relation to the graph of $y = mx + c$
- calculate the gradient and length of a line segment
- find the equation of a straight line in the form $y = mx + c$
- construct tables of values for $y = x^2 + ax + b$ and $y = -x^2 + ax + b$ and draw the corresponding parabolic graphs
- construct tables of values for $y = \frac{a}{x}$ and draw the corresponding hyperbolic graphs
- solve simultaneous equations graphically
- solve quadratic equations graphically.

A Straight line graphs

In Unit 1, we met pairs of quantities which are related to one another in such a way that they can be represented by a straight line graph. For example:
- the time a candle has been burning and the height of the candle
- the measure of a distance in miles and its measure in kilometres
- the measure of a temperature in °C and its measure in °F
- the time a workman takes to do a repair and the charge for the repair.

Mathematicians are interested in what these pairs of quantities have in common and they try to discover rules which apply to all of them. In other words, they will try to generalise.
The first step is to denote the two quantities by the letters x and y, instead of using h (for height) and t (for time) or
m (for miles) and k (for kilometres), etc.
The second step is to discover what relationships between x and y lead to a straight line graph when x and y are taken as cartesian coordinates.

Some relations and their graphs

Let us look at the relation $y = 2x + 1$.
We can take various values for x and calculate the corresponding values of y. For example,

when $x = 4$, the value of y is $8 + 1$ (that is 9)
and when $x = -3$, the value of y is $-6 + 1$ (that is -5)

It makes sense to choose the values of x in a systematic way and to present the corresponding values of x and y in a table. (With a relation as simple as $y = 2x + 1$, you can do the calculations in your head.)

x	-3	-2	-1	0	1	2	3	4
$y = 2x + 1$	-5	-3	-1	1	3	5	7	9

You can see from the table that, whenever x is increased by 1, the value of y increases by 2. (In fact, you can see from $y = 2x + 1$ that, whenever x is increased by an amount, the value of y increases by twice that amount.) This means that, when we plot points on a graph using (x, y) as cartesian coordinates, the graph rises at a constant rate – the points lie on a straight line.

The values of x do not need to be whole numbers. Provided the y value is obtained from $y = 2x + 1$, the corresponding point will lie on the line. For example, when $x = 2\frac{1}{2}$, the value of y is 6 and, as you can see on the graph, the point $(2\frac{1}{2}, 6)$ lies on the line.

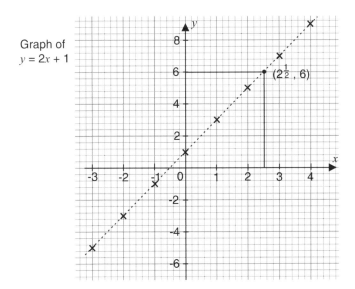

Graph of $y = 2x + 1$

Example 1

Make a table of values for the relation $y = \frac{1}{2}x - 1$ for values of x between -3 and 3. Draw the cartesian graph for this relation.

Solution

substitute the values of x to find the y-values

x	-3	-2	-1	0	1	2	3
$y = \frac{1}{2}x - 1$	$-2\frac{1}{2}$	-2	$-1\frac{1}{2}$	-1	$-\frac{1}{2}$	0	$\frac{1}{2}$

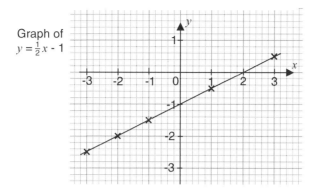

Graph of $y = \frac{1}{2}x - 1$

The 7 points obtained from the values in the table are shown as crosses.

The graph of $y = \frac{1}{2}x - 1$ is the straight line which has been drawn through these points.

Example 2

Make a table of values for the relation $y = 7 - 3x$ for values of x between -1 and 5. Draw the graph for this relation and write down the coordinates of the points where the graph crosses the x and y axes.

Solution

x	-1	0	1	2	3	4	5
$y = 7 - 3x$	10	7	4	1	-2	-5	-8

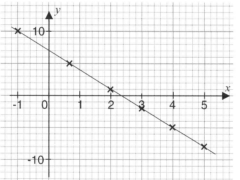

Graph of $y = 7 - 3x$

The graph crosses the y-axis at (0, 7) and the x-axis at (2.3, 0).

Example 3

Draw the graphs of $y = 3x + 4$ and $y = 2 - x$ on the same diagram, for values of x from -2 to 2. Write down the coordinates of the point where these two graphs intersect.

Solution

x	-2	-1	0	1	2
$y = 3x + 4$	-2	1	4	7	10

x	-2	-1	0	1	2
$y = 2 - x$	4	3	2	1	0

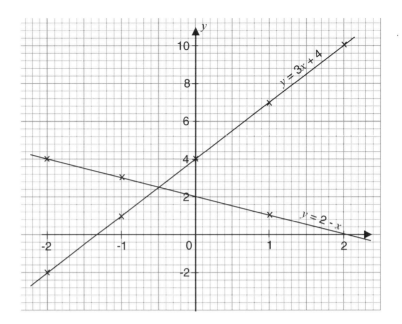

The two graphs are drawn in this diagram. Notice how they are labelled.

On the x-axis, 10 small squares (2 cm) represent 1 unit so each small square represents 0.1 unit.

On the y-axis, 10 small squares represent 4 units so each small square represents 0.4 unit.

The point at which the two graphs intersect (cross) has coordinates (−0.5, 2.5).

Example 4

Make a table of values for the relation $y = \dfrac{1}{(x+1)}$ for values of x from 0 to 4. Is the graph of this relation a straight line?

Solution

x	0	1	2	3	4
$y = \dfrac{1}{x+1}$	1	0.5	0.33	0.25	0.2

It is clear from the table that the values of y do not increase or decrease at a constant rate.

The corresponding points which are plotted in the diagram clearly do not lie on a straight line.

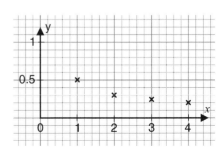

The points must not be joined up with straight line segments. The graph for this relation is, in fact, a curve.

Now try a few questions yourself.

EXERCISE 4

1. Complete the following table of values for the relation $y = \frac{x-2}{2}$ and draw the graph of the relation.

x	-2	0	2	4	6
$y = \frac{x-2}{2}$	-2				2

   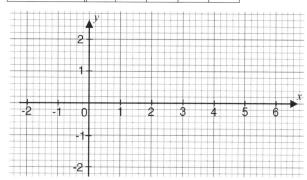

2. Make a table of values for the relation $y = 5 - 3x$ for whole number values of x from -2 to 4.

   Draw the graph of this relation and write down the coordinates of the point where it crosses the x-axis.

   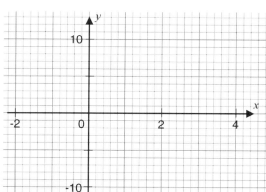

3. On the axes below, draw the graphs of $y = x - 1$ and $y = 4 - x$ for $-1 \leq x \leq 4$. Write down the coordinates of the point at which the graphs intersect.

   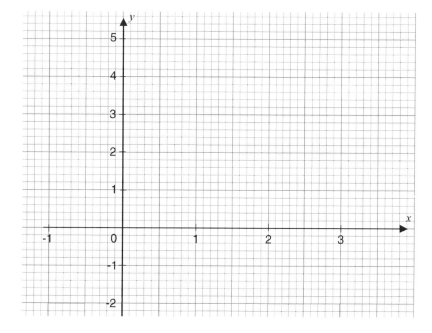

4. On the axes below, draw the graphs of the relations:

   a) $y = 2x$
   b) $y = 2x + 2$
   c) $y = 2x - 1$
   d) $y = 2x + 4$

   What do you notice about these graphs?

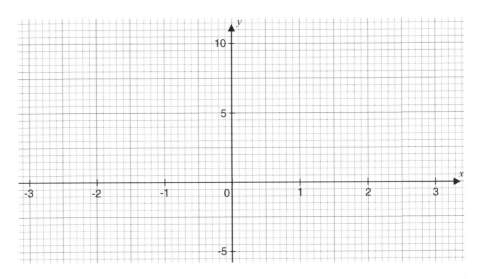

Check your answers at the end of this module.

Recognising relations which have straight line graphs

You may have realised by now that any relation of the form $y = mx + c$, where m and c are numbers, has a straight line graph. Whenever x is increased by 1, the value of y is increased by an amount m. More generally, if x is increased by any amount, y increases by m times that amount. The graph, therefore, rises at a constant rate — it must be a straight line.

Sometimes a relation is not given in the form $y = \ldots$ but is given in a form such as $3x + 4y = 12$. To see whether the graph of $3x + 4y = 12$ is a straight line, you must change it to the form $y = \ldots$ You will remember that, in Module 2 Unit 1, we said this was *changing the subject of the formula*.

For $3x + 4y = 12$
$$4y = 12 - 3x$$
$$y = 3 - \tfrac{3}{4}x$$
$$y = -\tfrac{3}{4}x + 3$$

This is $y = mx + c$ with $m = -\tfrac{3}{4}$ and $c = 3$.

It follows that the graph of $3x + 4y = 12$ is a straight line.

In general, any relation of the form $ax + by = k$ (where a, b and k are numbers) has a graph which is a straight line. (When we solved simultaneous equations in Module 2, we met equations such as $3x + 4y = 12$ and $x - 5y = 8$. These are **linear simultaneous equations**. You can now see why the word *linear* is used.)

To draw a straight line graph we only need to plot two points and join them. For reasons of accuracy, these two points should be as far apart as possible, and it is good practice to plot a third point (to check whether you have made a mistake in calculation or in plotting).

Lines parallel to one of the axes

Consider the line which is parallel to the y-axis and a distance c above it.

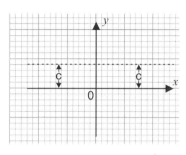

Every point on this line has a y-coordinate equal to c. In this case, the y-coordinate does not depend on the x-coordinate. The equation of the line is $y = c$.

The x-axis itself has the equation $y = 0$ (because every point on the x-axis has a y-coordinate equal to 0).

Consider now the line which is parallel to the y-axis and a distance d to the right of it, as shown in the diagram below.

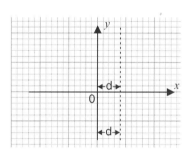

Every point on this line has an x-coordinate equal to d, no matter what its y-coordinate is. The equation of the line is $x = d$.

The y-axis itself has the equation $x = 0$ (because every point on the y-axis has an x-coordinate equal to 0).

The gradient of a straight line

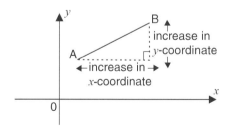

In Unit 1, when you were studying distance–time graphs, I defined the gradient of a straight line AB as

$$\frac{\text{increase in } y\text{-coordinate from A to B}}{\text{increase in } x\text{-coordinate from A to B}}$$

If you are given a straight line graph, you can choose *any* two points on it as A and B to find its gradient. This is because a straight line rises (or falls) at a constant rate.

In practice (for ease of calculation and to get an accurate result) you should try to choose two points as far apart as possible and such that the difference between their x-coordinates is a whole number.

When the equation of the straight line is known, it is possible to find its gradient without drawing the graph.

If the equation is in the form $y = mx + c$, we can see (as we mentioned before) that an increase of 1 in the value of x will result in an increase of m in the value of y. This means that:

> the gradient of the line $y = mx + c$ is m

For example, the gradient of the line $y = 2x - 1$ is 2
and the gradient of the line $y = 10 - \frac{1}{2}x$ is $-\frac{1}{2}$

> the gradient is the coefficient of x

If the equation of the line is in a different form, we must *change the subject of the formula* to y.

For example, to find the gradient of the line $2x + 5y = 7$, we work as follows:

$2x + 5y = 7$
$5y = 7 - 2x$
$y = \frac{7}{5} - \frac{2}{5}x$

The gradient of this line is the coefficient of x (the number in front of x) in the equation.

Hence, the gradient of the line $2x + 5y = 7$ is $-\frac{2}{5}$.

Parallel lines

Parallel lines are lines which have the same gradient. The lines $y = 5x$ and $y = 5x + 4$ are parallel (each has a gradient of 5). The lines
$3x - 4y = 2$ and $8y - 6x = 9$ are parallel (the first one is $y = \frac{3}{4}x - \frac{1}{2}$ and the second is $y = \frac{3}{4}x + \frac{9}{8}$ so each has a gradient of $\frac{3}{4}$).

Example 1

Draw the straight line $3y - 2x = 12$ and find its gradient.

Solution

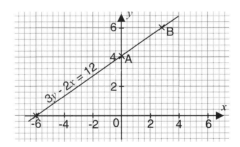

Putting $x = 0$, we get $3y = 12$, so $y = 4$.
   Therefore $(0, 4)$ is on the line.
Putting $y = 0$, we get $-2x = 12$, so $x = -6$.
   Therefore $(-6, 0)$ is on the line.
For a check point I put $x = 3$ and get
   $3y = 18$, so $y = 6$.
   Therefore $(3, 6)$ is on the line.

> You can choose any x and substitute it into the equation to find y. (x, y) will be a point on the line.

The line is drawn in the diagram.
To find its gradient, we can take the two points A (0, 4) and B (3, 6) and say gradient = $\frac{\text{increase in } y}{\text{increase in } x} = \frac{6-4}{3-0} = \frac{2}{3}$. Check that you would get the same gradient if you chose two different points on the line.

Example 2

Find the gradient of the line $5x + 4y - 8 = 0$.

Solution

In this question, you are not asked to draw the line and, in fact, you do not need to draw it since only the gradient has to be found. You can *change the subject of the formula* as follows:

$$5x + 4y - 8 = 0$$
$$4y = 8 - 5x$$
$$y = 2 - \frac{5}{4}x$$

The equation is now in the form $y = mx + c$ and m is the gradient. Hence, the gradient of the line $5x + 4y - 8 = 0$ is $-\frac{5}{4}$.

Example 3

Find the gradient of the straight line graph shown in this diagram.

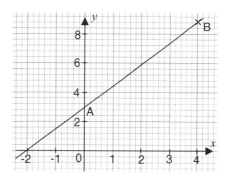

Solution

You must first choose two points, A and B, on the line. I will take A to be (0, 3) and B to be (4, 9).

Gradient of the line = $\frac{\text{increase in } y\text{-coordinate from A to B}}{\text{increase in } x\text{-coordinate from A to B}}$

$$= \frac{9-3}{4-0} = \frac{6}{4} = \frac{3}{2}$$

Note: If I had taken A to be (−2, 0) and B to be (4, 9), the calculation would have been gradient = $\frac{9-0}{4-(-2)} = \frac{9}{6} = \frac{3}{2}$.

Example 4

The coordinates of the points P and Q are (−3, −1) and (2, 1) respectively. Find the gradient of the line PQ.

Solution

First, draw a diagram (it need not be very accurate).

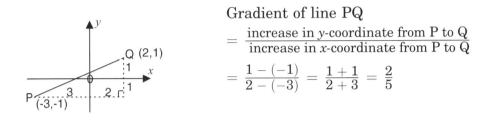

Gradient of line PQ

$$= \frac{\text{increase in } y\text{-coordinate from P to Q}}{\text{increase in } x\text{-coordinate from P to Q}}$$

$$= \frac{1-(-1)}{2-(-3)} = \frac{1+1}{2+3} = \frac{2}{5}$$

Note: This question can be done without drawing. The working would be:

$$\text{Gradient} = \frac{y\text{-coordinate of P} - y\text{-coordinate of Q}}{x\text{-coordinate of P} - x\text{-coordinate of Q}}$$

$$= \frac{1-(-1)}{2-(-3)}$$

$$= \frac{1+1}{2+3} = \frac{2}{5}$$

You should now understand how to find the gradient of a straight line from its equation or from the coordinates of two points on it. Test your understanding by answering the following questions.

EXERCISE 5

1. Draw the straight line $4x + 5y = 20$ and find its gradient.

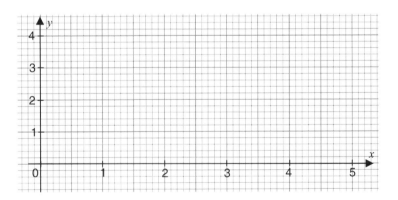

2. Find the gradient of each of the straight lines:
   a) $3x - 4y = 24$
   b) $4x + 5y + 6 = 0$
   c) $x = 2y + 3$

3. Show that the lines $2x = 4y + 3$ and $6y - 3x + 5 = 0$ are parallel.

4. Given the points P $(0, 4)$ and Q $(2, -1)$, calculate the gradient of the line PQ.

5. Find the gradient of this straight line graph.

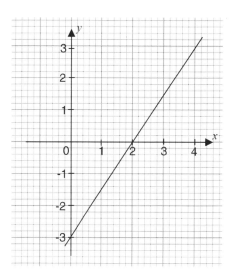

Check your answers at the end of this module.

Interpreting the equation $y = mx + c$

You know that the graph of $y = mx + c$ is a straight line and that m (the coefficient of x) is the gradient of that straight line. Remember the following important facts about gradients:

The greater the value of m the steeper the line.

If m is positive, the line slopes upwards from left to right.

If m is zero, the line is horizontal (it is parallel to the x-axis).

If m is negative, the line slopes downwards from left to right.

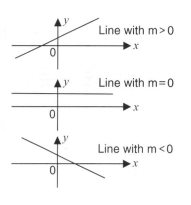

What does the value of c (the constant in the equation $y = mx + c$) tell us about the straight line?

Putting $x = 0$ in $y = mx + c$ gives $y = c$, so the point $(0, c)$ is on the line. This means that the line crosses the y-axis at a point which is c units above or below the origin (depending on whether c is a positive or negative number).

---

c is called the **intercept on the y-axis** of the line $y = mx + c$.
This is sometimes shortened to ***y-intercept***.

Example 1

For the line $2y - 3x = 12$, find the gradient and the intercept on the y-axis.

Solution

You must first put the equation in the form $y = mx + c$:
$$2y - 3x = 12$$
$$2y = 3x + 12$$
$$y = \tfrac{3}{2}x + 6$$

The gradient of the line $= \tfrac{3}{2}$ and the intercept on the y-axis $= 6$.

Example 2

Write down and simplify the equation of the line which has a gradient of $-\tfrac{1}{2}$ and a y-intercept of 3.

Solution

The equation of the line is $y = mx + c$ where $m = -\tfrac{1}{2}$ and $c = 3$.
The equation is $y = -\tfrac{1}{2}x + 3$ which is $2y = -x + 6$.
The equation could also be written as $x + 2y = 6$.

Example 3

Find the gradient and the intercept on the y-axis of the line drawn in this diagram and use them to find the equation of the line.

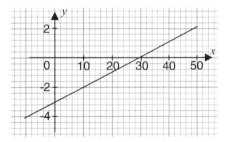

Solution

The intercept on the y-axis is half-way between -2 and -4, so it is -3. To find the gradient, take the points $(0, -3)$ and $(30, 0)$ which are on the line.

Gradient $= \dfrac{\text{increase in } y\text{-coordinate}}{\text{increase in } x\text{-coordinate}} = \dfrac{3}{30} = \dfrac{1}{10}$.

> notice that you can see from the diagram that the gradient is positive

The equation of the line is $y = mx + c$ where $m = \tfrac{1}{10}$ and $c = -3$.
Hence, the equation of the line is $y = \tfrac{x}{10} - 3$.
This could be written as $10y = x - 30$.

Example 4

Find the equation of the line through the points P $(2, 1)$ and Q $(6, 9)$.

Solution

Gradient of line PQ $= \dfrac{y\text{-coordinate of Q} - y\text{-coordinate of P}}{x\text{-coordinate of Q} - x\text{-coordinate of P}}$
$= \dfrac{9-1}{6-2} = \dfrac{8}{4} = 2$

The equation of the line is $y = mx + c$ where $m = 2$.
The equation is, therefore, $y = 2x + c$.

You haven't been told where the line cuts the y-axis so you don't know what c's value is. You can find it though, by using the fact that the points P and Q are on the line.

The line passes through P so its coordinates (2, 1) must satisfy the equation.

Hence $1 = 4 + c$
So $c = -3$

> you could also have used the point Q to find the value of c

The equation of the line is $y = 2x - 3$.

Try the following questions.

EXERCISE 6

1. For each of the following lines, find the gradient and the intercept on the y-axis:
   a) $y = 4 - 3x$
   b) $2y - 4 = x$
   c) $x + y = 3$

2. Write down and simplify the equation of the line which has:
   a) a gradient of $\frac{3}{5}$ and a y-intercept of -2
   b) a gradient of $-\frac{1}{2}$ and a y-intercept of $\frac{3}{4}$

3. Find the gradient and the intercept on the y-axis for the line drawn in each of the following diagrams, and hence find the equation of each line.
   a)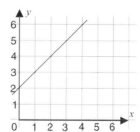
   b)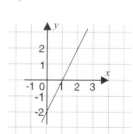
   c)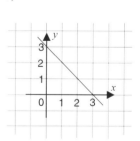

4. Find the equation of the line through the points P (5, 2) and Q (7, 8).

Check your answers at the end of this module.

The length of a line segment

I have described how to find the gradient of a line, including how to find the gradient of the straight line joining two points (this is called a line segment).

It is also possible to find the length of a line segment. To do this, you need to know Pythagoras's theorem. This is one of the best-known results in mathematics and you have probably met it before.

Pythagoras's theorem tells us that there is a simple, but surprising, connection between the lengths of the sides of a right-angled triangle.

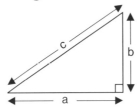

If c is the length of the longest side (the hypotenuse) and a and b are the lengths of the other two sides, then

$c^2 = a^2 + b^2$.

We shall meet this again in Module 5 and see how it could be proved.

Let me show you how to use Pythagoras's theorem to find the length of a line segment, for example, the line segment joining the point P (2, 4) to the point Q (14, 9).

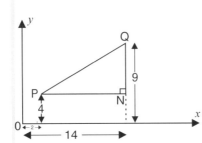

First draw a sketch to show the line segment PQ. Can you see that the vertical distance between P and Q $= 9 - 4 = 5$ and the horizontal distance between P and Q $= 14 - 2 = 12$?

In the diagram, triangle PNQ has a right-angle at N, so you can use Pythagoras's theorem:

$(PQ)^2 = (QN)^2 + (PN)^2$
$= 25 + 144$
$= 169$

So, the length of the line segment PQ $= \sqrt{169} = 13$ units.

Example 1

In triangle ABC, angle B is a right-angle, side AB = 7 and side BC = 24. Calculate the length of side AC.

Solution

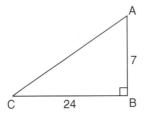

Using Pythagoras's theorem:
$(AC)^2 = (AB)^2 + (BC)^2$
$= 49 + 576$
$= 625$
Side AC $= \sqrt{625}$
$= 15$

don't forget to find the square root

Example 2

Given the points P (–2, 5) and Q (4, –3), calculate the length of the line segment PQ.

Solution

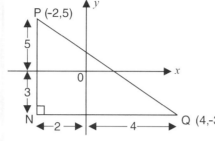

The points P and Q, and their distances from the axes, are shown in the sketch.

Triangle PNQ has a right-angle at N so we can use Pythagoras's theorem:
$$(PQ)^2 = (PN)^2 + (NQ)^2$$
$$= (5+3)^2 + (2+4)^2$$
$$= 64 + 36$$
$$= 100$$
$$\text{Length PQ} = \sqrt{100}$$
$$= 10$$

Example 3

Given the points S $(-3, -2)$ and T $(4, 1)$, calculate the length of the line segment ST.

Solution

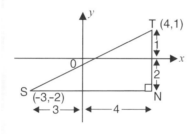

In the sketch, triangle SNT has a right-angle at N so we can use Pythagoras's theorem:
$$(ST)^2 = (SN)^2 + (NT)^2$$
$$= (3+4)^2 + (2+1)^2$$
$$= 49 + 9$$
$$= 58$$
$$\text{Length ST} = \sqrt{58}$$
$$= 7.62 \text{ to 3 significant figures.}$$

Practise using Pythagoras's theorem by doing the following exercise.

EXERCISE 7

1. In triangle DEF, angle D is a right-angle, side DE = 8 and side DF = 15. Calculate the length of side EF.

2. Given the points A $(-4, 2)$ and B $(5, 14)$, calculate the length of the line segment AB.

3. Given the points C $(-4, -10)$ and D $(6, 14)$, calculate the length of the line segment CD.

4. Given the points G $(-2, 3)$ and H $(4, 12)$, calculate the length of the line segment GH.

Check your answers at the end of this module.

B Some curved graphs

You have seen that any relation of the form $ax + by = k$ has a graph which is a straight line, and vice versa, that any straight line graph represents a relation of the form $ax + by = k$.

In this section we shall consider relations of the form $y = x^2 + ax + b$, $y = -x^2 + ax + b$ and $y = \frac{a}{x}$. The graphs of these relations cannot be straight lines. As we shall see, they are curves.

Functions

Most of the relations you have to study in the IGCSE course are of a particular type known as **functions**.

> The variable y is said to be a **function** of the variable x if, for each value of x, there is one and only one value of y.

If the relation between x and y is $3x + y = 6$, then y is a function of x (because $y = 6 - 3x$ and there is a unique value of y for each value of x). Notice also that, in this case, x is a function of y (because $x = 2 - \frac{y}{3}$ and there is a unique value of x for each value of y).

However, if the relation between x and y is $y^2 - x^2 = 9$, then y is *not* a function of x because $y = \pm \sqrt{9 + x^2}$ so there are *two* values of y for each value of x.

Note: The wording in graphical questions may vary slightly and you should be aware that the following instructions all mean the same thing.
'Draw the graph of the function $y = x^2 - 3x + 2$.'
'Draw the graph whose equation is $y = x^2 - 3x + 2$.'
'Draw the graph of $y = x^2 - 3x + 2$.'
'Draw the graph of the relation $y = x^2 - 3x + 2$.'

Quadratic graphs

The relations $y = x^2 + ax + b$ and $y = -x^2 + ax + b$ are **quadratic functions**. As we draw the graphs of these functions for various values of the constants a and b, you will become aware that they all have a particular shape – they have a family resemblance to one-another.

Example 1

Draw the graph of the function $y = x^2$ for values of x from -3 to 3.

Solution

$y = x^2$ is the simplest of the quadratic functions.
Start by considering whole number values of x:

x	-3	-2	-1	0	1	2	3
$y = x^2$	9	4	1	0	1	4	9

Remember that (negative) × (negative) = (positive).
So if $x = -3$ then $y = (-3)^2 = (-3) \times (-3) = +9$.

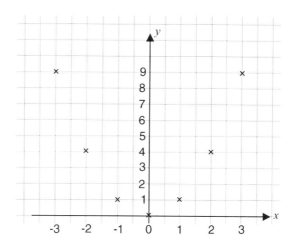

The corresponding points are shown in the diagram. They clearly do not lie on a straight line.

To obtain a better idea of the shape of the graph, we use some fractional or decimal values of x to find more points on the graph.

x	-2.5	-1.5	-0.5	0.5	1.5	2.5
$y = x^2$	6.25	2.25	0.25	0.25	2.25	6.25

The values of x and y have been used to plot six more points in the diagram.

The shape of the graph is now clearer.

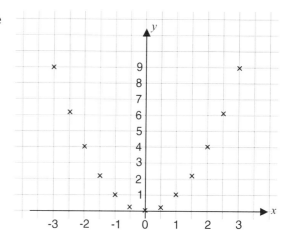

As you plot more and more points, you can see that the graph is curved all the way along its length. No part of the graph is straight.

> it follows that you should not use a ruler to draw any part of the graph

The graph of $y = x^2$ is a curve called a **parabola**.

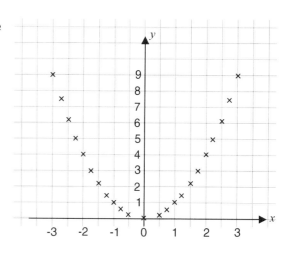

Example 2

Draw the graph of the function $y = x^2 + 2x - 1$ for values of x from -4 to 2.

Solution

You may find it difficult to work out the values of $x^2 + 2x - 1$ in your head. If so, you could arrange the work as follows:

$$y = x^2 + 2x - 1$$
When $x = 2$, $y = 4 + 4 - 1 = 7$
When $x = 1$, $y = 1 + 2 - 1 = 2$
When $x = 0$, $y = 0 + 0 - 1 = -1$
When $x = -1$, $y = 1 - 2 - 1 = -2$
When $x = -2$, $y = 4 - 4 - 1 = -1$
When $x = -3$, $y = 9 - 6 - 1 = 2$
When $x = -4$, $y = 16 - 8 - 1 = 7$

A different way to write this is to use a table:

x	-4	-3	-2	-1	0	1	2
x^2	16	9	4	1	0	1	4
$+2x$	-8	-6	-4	-2	0	$+2$	$+4$
-1	-1	-1	-1	-1	-1	-1	-1
$y = x^2 + 2x - 1$	7	2	-1	-2	-1	2	7

The values of x and y in the table have been used to obtain seven points marked on the graph. These points have been joined by a smooth curve.

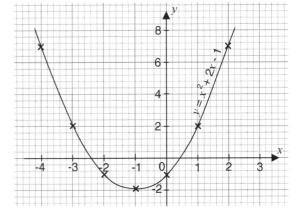

Example 3

Draw the graph of the function $y = x^2 - 3x$ for values of x from -2 to 5.

Solution

We use the table method to find the values of y.

x	-2	-1	0	1	2	3	4	5
x^2	4	1	0	1	4	9	16	25
$-3x$	$+6$	$+3$	0	-3	-6	-9	-12	-15
$y = x^2 - 3x$	10	4	0	-2	-2	0	4	10

The values of x and y have been used to obtain the eight points marked on the graph and a smooth curve has been drawn through them.

Notice that the lowest point on the graph is where $x = 1.5$. It is worth working out the value of y at this point.
It is $y = 2.25 - 4.5$
$\phantom{\text{It is }y} = -2.25$

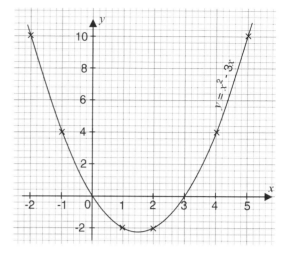

Example 4

Draw the graph of the function $y = 6 + x - x^2$ for values of x from -3 to 4.

Solution

x	-3	-2	-1	0	1	2	3	4
6	6	6	6	6	6	6	6	6
$+x$	-3	-2	-1	0	$+1$	$+2$	$+3$	$+4$
$-x^2$	-9	-4	-1	0	-1	-4	-9	-16
$y = 6 + x - x^2$	-6	0	4	6	6	4	0	-6

The graph of $y = 6 + x - x^2$ is drawn here. The highest point on this graph is where $x = 0.5$ and the corresponding value of $y = 6 + 0.5 - 0.25$
$\phantom{\text{value of }y} = 6.25$

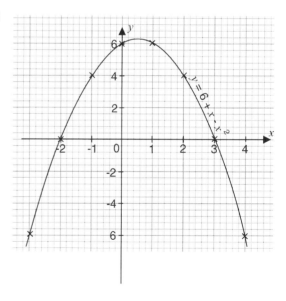

You will have noticed that the graphs of $y = x^2 + 2x - 1$ and $y = x^2 - 3x$ have the same general shape as the graph of $y = x^2$. They are all parabolas. The graph of $y = 6 + x - x^2$ is also a parabola but it is 'upside down' (because it contains $-x^2$ instead of x^2).

You should remember this whenever you are asked to draw a graph of a function of the form $y = x^2 + ax + b$ or $y = -x^2 + ax + b$.

Hints on drawing curves
1. Always use a sharp pencil – do not use a pen (you may make a mistake and want to replace part of the curve).
2. Make sure that you have plotted a sufficient number of points – usually 7 or 8 points will be enough. If there is a large gap between two points, plot an extra point between them.
3. If a plotted point does not seem to lie on the curve through the other points, look for an error in your table of values. (Do not alter your curve to go through a point which is obviously wrong.)

Time now for you to draw some graphs for yourself. Just one hint – all the curves are parabolas!

EXERCISE 8

1. Make a table of values and draw the graph of the function $y = x^2 + 2x$ for values of x from -4 to 2.

x	-4	-3	-2	-1	0	1	2
x^2							
$+2x$							
$y = x^2 + 2x$							

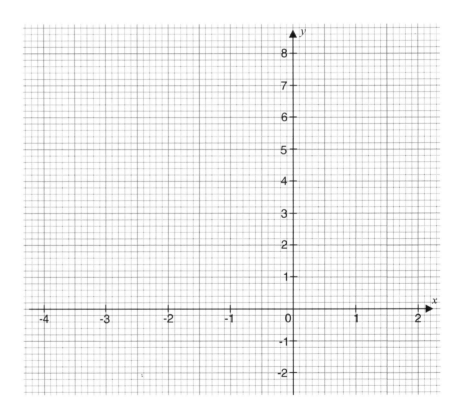

2. Make a table of values and draw the graph of the function $y = x^2 - 5x - 4$ for values of x from -2 to 7.
   Write down the coordinates of the lowest point on the graph.

x	-2	-1	0	1	2	3	4	5	6	7
x^2										
$-5x$										
-4										
$y = x^2 - 5x - 4$										

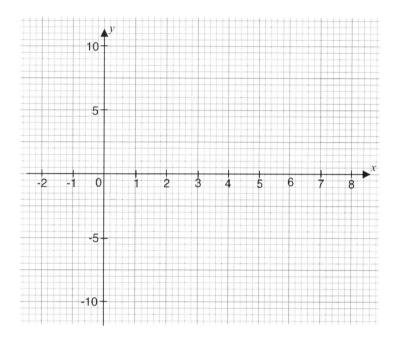

3. Draw the graph of the function $y = 4 - x^2$ for values of x from -3 to 3.

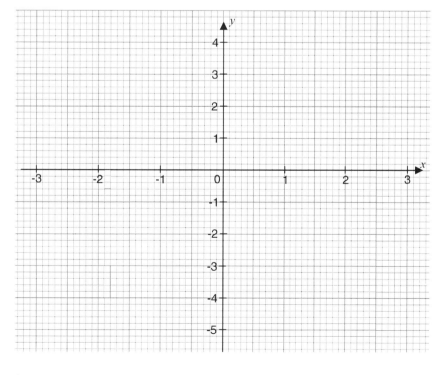

Check your answers at the end of this module.

Graphs of reciprocal functions ($y = \frac{a}{x}$)

Let's investigate how the graph of $y = \frac{6}{x}$ differs from the graphs we have drawn so far in this module.

First of all, notice that there is no value of y corresponding to $x = 0$. To work out $6 \div 0$ you would have to find a number which, when multiplied by 0, gives an answer of 6. This is impossible because *any* number multiplied by 0 gives an answer of 0.

Taking some positive whole number values of x, I obtain the following table:

x	1	2	3	4	5	6
$y = \frac{6}{x}$	6	3	2	1.5	1.2	1

When I plot the corresponding points, it is clear that they do not lie on a straight line.

If I draw a curve through the points, it is different from the curves I obtained for $y = x^2 + ax + b$ and $y = -x^2 + ax + b$.

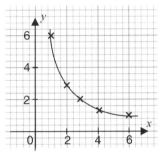

In fact, I have drawn only part of the graph, because I still have to consider negative values of x.

Here is a table for some negative whole number values of x.

remember that (positive) ÷ (negative) = (negative)

x	-6	-5	-4	-3	-2	-1
$y = \frac{6}{x}$	-1	-1.2	-1.5	-2	-3	-6

I now have a more complete picture of the graph. It is clear now that this curve is in two separate pieces. (The graphs of $ax + by = k$, $y = x^2 + ax + b$ and $y = -x^2 + ax + b$ were in one piece.)

Each piece of the curve gets closer and closer to the x-axis as the value of x increases (numerically) but the graph never meets the x-axis. (This is because, when x is very large, $\frac{6}{x}$ is very small but never zero.)

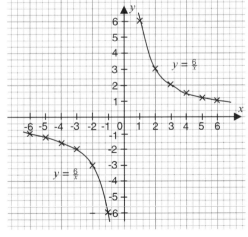

Each piece of the curve gets closer and closer to the y-axis as the value of x approaches zero, but the graph never meets the y-axis. (This is because there is no value of y for $x = 0$.)

The type of curve we obtain from the reciprocal function $y = \frac{a}{x}$ is called a **rectangular hyperbola**. It was studied (along with the parabola) by the ancient Greeks in the 4th century BC.

Example

Draw the graph of the function $y = -\frac{12}{x}$ $(x \neq 0)$ for $-12 \leq x \leq 12$.

Solution

When making the table of values, remember that
(negative) ÷ (negative) = (positive) and
(negative) ÷ (positive) = (negative).

x	-12	-11	-10	-9	-8	-7	-6	-5	-4	-3	-2	-1
$y = -\frac{12}{x}$	1	1.1	1.2	1.3	1.5	1.7	2	2.4	3	4	6	12

x	1	2	3	4	5	6	7	8	9	10	11	12
$y = -\frac{12}{x}$	-12	-6	-4	-3	-2.4	-2	-1.7	-1.5	-1.3	-1.2	-1.1	-1

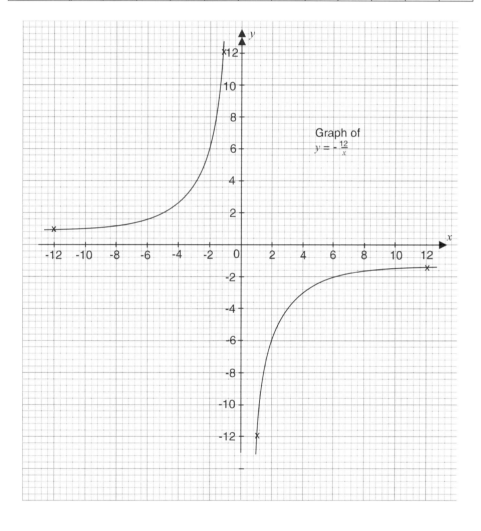

Graph of $y = -\frac{12}{x}$

Notice that the graph of $y = -\frac{12}{x}$ is the same shape as the graph of $y = \frac{6}{x}$ but the two pieces of $y = -\frac{12}{x}$ are in the top left and bottom right quarters of the graph paper, whereas the two pieces of $y = \frac{6}{x}$ are in the bottom left and top right quarters. This is because $y = -\frac{12}{x}$ has a negative value of 'a' and $y = \frac{6}{x}$ has a positive value of 'a' in the general function $y = \frac{a}{x}$.

C Using graphs to solve equations

Solving simultaneous equations graphically

In Module 2 Unit 4, you learned how to solve simultaneous equations by using a *substitution method* and by using a method of *equal coefficients*. The equations we dealt with in Module 2 should be called *linear simultaneous equations in two unknowns*. You will see why the word *linear* is appropriate when we solve such equations by a graphical method.

Example 1

Use a graphical method to solve the simultaneous equations
$y = x + 3, \quad x + y = 2$.

Solution

First draw the graphs of $y = x + 3$ and $x + y = 2$ on the same diagram. Each of these graphs is a straight line, so we shall plot 3 points for each of them (2 points to fix the line and the third point as a check).

$y = x + 3$

x	−4	0	4
y	−1	3	7

$x + y = 2$

x	−4	0	4
y	6	2	−2

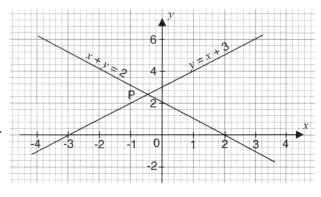

The point P where the lines cross has coordinates $(-0.5, 2.5)$. This is the only point which is on both lines.

This means that the pair of values $x = -0.5$, $y = 2.5$ satisfies $y = x + 3$ and $x + y = 2$ simultaneously.

In other words, the solution of the simultaneous equations
$y = x + 3, \quad x + y = 2$
is $x = -0.5, \ y = 2.5$

Example 2

The diagram has been drawn to solve a pair of simultaneous equations. Write down the solution of the equations and check it by substituting in both equations.

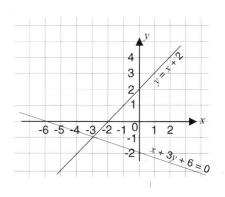

Solution

The lines cross at the point $(-3, -1)$ and so the solution of the equations $x + 3y + 6 = 0$ and $y = x + 2$ is $x = -3$, $y = -1$.

Check: When $x = -3$ and $y = -1$,
$x + 3y + 6 = -3 - 3 + 6 = 0$ ✓
and $x + 2 = -3 + 2 = -1 = y$ ✓ } The solution is checked.

Example 3

Use a graphical method to solve the simultaneous equations
$3x + 4y = 12$, $x - 2y + 2 = 0$.

Solution

The line $3x + 4y = 12$ crosses the y-axis where $x = 0$ and $y = 3$, that is at the point $(0, 3)$. Similarly, the line crosses the x-axis at the point $(4, 0)$. These two points have been plotted in the diagram and joined to form the line $3x + 4y = 12$.
The line $x - 2y + 2 = 0$ crosses the y-axis at the point $(0, 1)$ and the x-axis at $(-2, 0)$.

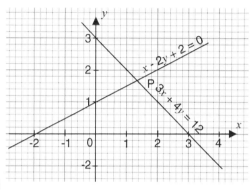

From the diagram, the solution of the simultaneous equations
$3x + 4y = 12$ and $x - 2y + 2 = 0$ is $x = 1.6$, $y = 1.8$

If you were asked to solve some linear simultaneous equations, you would probably choose to use the *substitution method* or the method of *equal coefficients*. These methods will give the exact values of x and y, and take no longer than the graphical method.

However, you are expected to be able to use the graphical method, partly because it can be used to solve simultaneous equations which are not linear and for which there is no exact solution.

EXERCISE 9

1. Use a graphical method to solve the simultaneous equations $y = 2x + 4$, $x + y = 1$. (Take values of x from -3 to 3.)

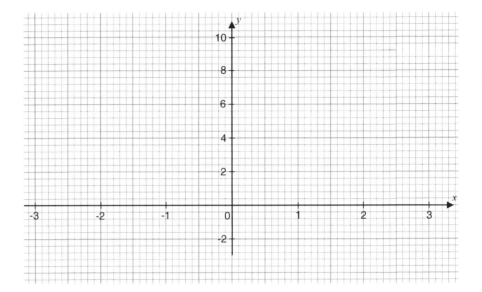

2. Use a graphical method to solve the simultaneous equations $y = 2x - 5$, $2y = x + 2$. (Take values of x from 0 to 6.)

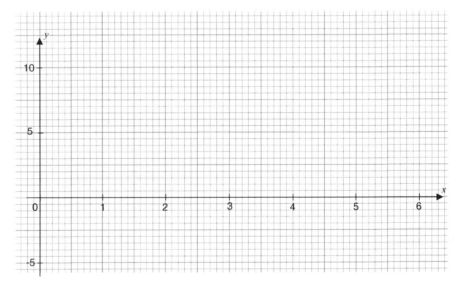

3. Each of the diagrams below gives the solution of a pair of simultaneous equations. In each case, write down the solution of the simultaneous equations and check it by substituting in both equations.

a)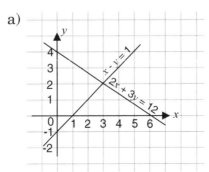
b)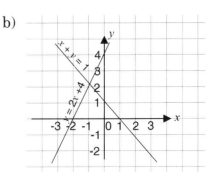

Solving quadratic (and other) equations graphically

Check your answers at the end of this module. Alternatively, you could check them by solving the simultaneous equations by the substitution method or by the method of equal coefficients!

Suppose you were asked to solve the equation $x^2 - 3x - 1 = 0$. That means, find the value, or values, of x which make $x^2 - 3x - 1$ equal to 0.

You could try a few values of x, for example:

when $x = 0$, $x^2 - 3x - 1 = 0 - 0 - 1 = -1$
when $x = 1$, $x^2 - 3x - 1 = 1 - 3 - 1 = -3$
when $x = 2$, $x^2 - 3x - 1 = 4 - 6 - 1 = -3$
when $x = 3$, $x^2 - 3x - 1 = 9 - 9 - 1 = -1$
when $x = 4$, $x^2 - 3x - 1 = 16 - 12 - 1 = 3$

The value of $x^2 - 3x - 1$ is below 0 when $x = 3$, and above 0 when $x = 4$. It appears that there is a value of x between 3 and 4 which makes $x^2 - 3x - 1$ equal to 0.

Try $x = 3.5$. $x^2 - 3x - 1 = 12.25 - 10.5 - 1 = 0.75$.
It now appears that there is a value of x between 3 and 3.5 which makes $x^2 - 3x - 1$ equal to 0.

We could go on substituting values for x, but you will have realised by now that the work we are doing is the same as we do to draw the graph of $y = x^2 - 3x - 1$. We can, in fact, solve the equation $x^2 - 3x - 1 = 0$ by using the graph of $y = x^2 - 3x - 1$.

The graph is shown in the diagram below. To solve the equation $x^2 - 3x - 1 = 0$ we must find the point, or points, on the curve which have a y-value of zero. In other words, we must find where the curve crosses the x-axis.

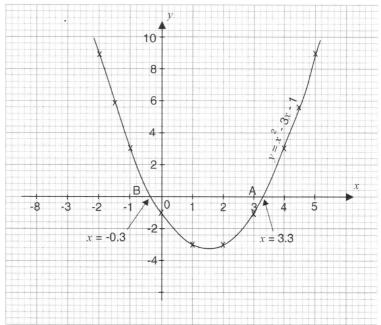

As you can see, this curve crosses the x-axis at two points, A and B. The x-values at these points are 3.3 and -0.3 respectively.

It follows that the solutions of the quadratic equation $x^2 - 3x - 1 = 0$ are $x = 3.3$ and $x = -0.3$.

Example 1

Use the graph of $y = x^2 - 2x - 7$ to solve the equations:
  a) $x^2 - 2x - 7 = 0$
  b) $x^2 - 2x - 7 = 3$
  c) $x^2 - 2x = 1$

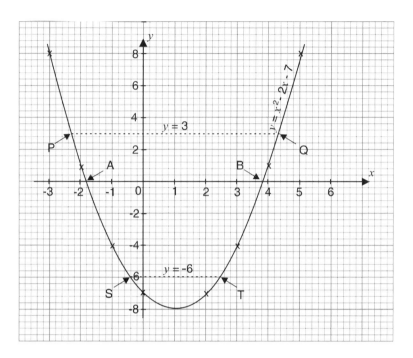

Solution

a) We have to find the points on the curve which have a y-coordinate of 0. There are two such points, marked A and B on the graph. The x-coordinates of these points are -1.8 and 3.8, so the solutions of the equation $x^2 - 2x - 7 = 0$ are $x = -1.8$ and $x = 3.8$.

b) We have to find the points on the curve which have a y-coordinate of 3. There are two such points, marked P and Q on the graph. The x-coordinates of these points are -2.3 and 4.3, so the solutions of the equation $x^2 - 2x - 7 = 3$ are $x = -2.3$ and $x = 4.3$.

c) We must first re-arrange the equation $x^2 - 2x = 1$ so that the left-hand side matches the function whose graph we are using. Taking 7 from both sides, we get $x^2 - 2x - 7 = 1 - 7$
that is $x^2 - 2x - 7 = -6$.

We can now proceed as we did in parts a) and b).
We find the points on the curve which have a y-coordinate of -6. They are marked S and T on the graph. Their x-coordinates are -0.4 and 2.4. The solutions of the equation $x^2 - 2x = 1$ are $x = -0.4$ and $x = 2.4$.

Example 2

a) Use the graph of $y = \frac{8}{x}$ to solve the equation $\frac{8}{x} = 5.7$.

b) On the diagram, draw the graph of $y = x$ and hence find a value of x such that $\frac{8}{x} = x$.

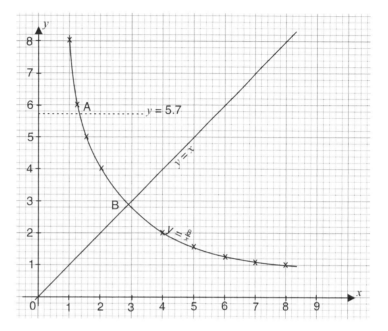

Solution

a) We have to find a point on the curve which has a y-coordinate of 5.7. The point is marked A on the diagram. Its x-coordinate is 1.4 so the solution of the equation $\frac{8}{x} = 5.7$ is $x = 1.4$.

b) The straight line $y = x$ crosses the curve $y = \frac{8}{x}$ at the point B whose x-coordinate is 2.8. Hence, a value of x such that $\frac{8}{x} = x$ is 2.8.

EXERCISE 10

1. Use this graph of the function $y = x^2 - x - 2$ to solve the equations:
   a) $x^2 - x - 2 = 0$
   b) $x^2 - x - 2 = 6$
   c) $x^2 - x = 6$

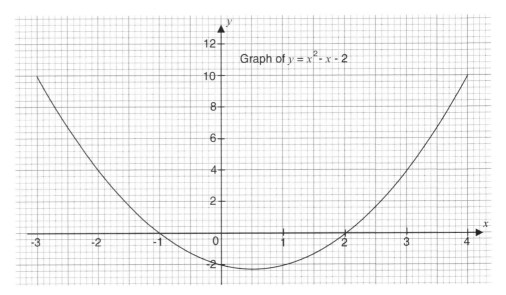

2. A man makes a journey of 240km. His average speed is x kilometres per hour and the time the journey takes is y hours.
   a) Complete this table of corresponding values of x and y.

x	20	40	60	80	100	120
y	12		4			2

   b) On the axes below, draw a graph to represent the relation between x and y.
   c) Write down the relation between x and y in its algebraic form.

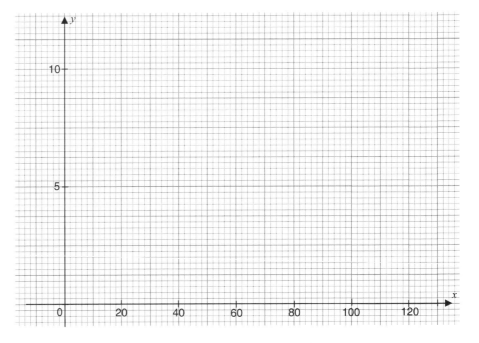

Check your answers at the end of this module.

You have now reached the end of Unit 2 and, if you are studying the CORE syllabus only (and not the EXTENDED syllabus), you have reached the end of Module 3.

Summary

In this unit you learnt about straight line graphs and that:

- $ax + by = k$ or $y = mx + c$ is the general form of a straight line graph
- a line parallel to the y-axis has equation $x = c$
- a line parallel to the x-axis has equation $y = c$
- parallel straight lines have equal gradients
- to draw a straight line graph, plot 2 points (and a third one to check).

If you are studying the EXTENDED syllabus you also learnt that:

- m is the gradient of a straight line graph
- c is the y-intercept of a straight line graph
- you can use Pythagoras's theorem to calculate the length of a line segment.

You continued by learning:

- how to draw parabolas of the form $y = x^2 + ax + b$ or $y = -x^2 + ax + b$ by plotting points
- how to draw graphs of reciprocal functions ($y = \frac{a}{x}$) by plotting points
- how to solve simultaneous equations by drawing their graphs and reading their point of intersection
- how to solve quadratic equations by drawing the graph.

Check your progress

1. a) (i) On the grid below, plot the points (−6, −2), (−4, 0), (−2, 2) and (0, 4). Draw a straight line through the four points.
   (ii) Find the gradient of the straight line that you have drawn.

   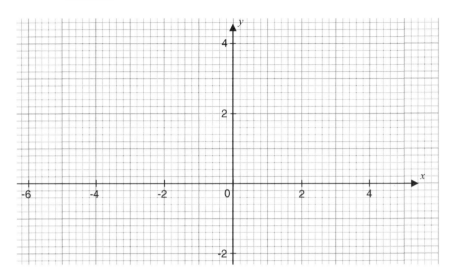

   b) (i) If $y = \frac{1}{3}x + 2$, fill in the blanks in the table of values below.

x	−6	−3		3
y	0		2	

   (ii) Draw the graph of $y = \frac{1}{3}x + 2$ on the grid above.

   c) Write down the coordinates of the point at which the two graphs meet.

2.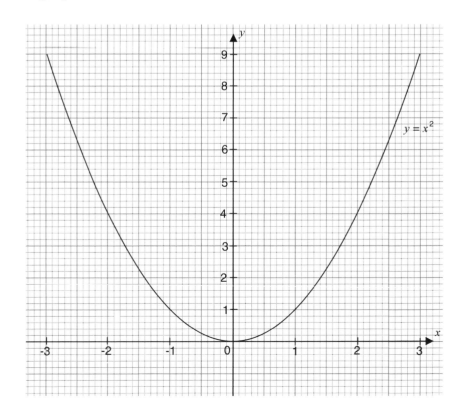

The graph of $y = x^2$ is drawn on the grid on the previous page.

a) The table shows some corresponding values of x and y for the function $y = x^2 + 3$.

x	-2	-1.5	-1	-0.5	0	0.5	1	1.5	2
y		5.25	4	3.25	3		4	5.25	7

Work out the missing values of y, and put them in the table.

b) Plot the points on the grid on the previous page and join them up with a smooth curve.
c) Will the two curves ever meet? Explain your answer.
d) By drawing a suitable straight line on the grid, solve the equations:
   (i) $x^2 = 6$
   (ii) $x^2 + 3 = 6$

3.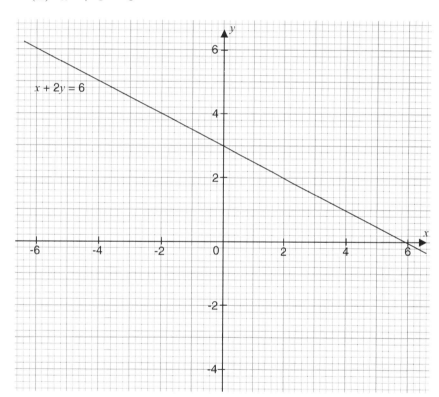

The graph of $x + 2y = 6$ is drawn on the grid above.

a) Find the gradient of the straight line $x + 2y = 6$.

b) (i) If $y = \frac{3}{2}x - 3$, complete the table below.

x	0	2	4
y			

   (ii) Draw the graph of $y = \frac{3}{2}x - 3$ on the grid above.

c) Solve the simultaneous equations $x + 2y = 6$, $y = \frac{3}{2}x - 3$.

4. a) Calculate the distance between the points C (7, 4) and S (11, 1).

    b) An ant crawls around the circumference of a circle centre C, radius 3. What is its greatest distance from a spider at S?

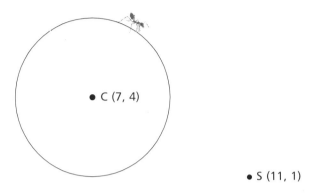

Check your answers at the end of this module.

Unit 3
Other Algebraic Graphs

By now, you should know how to draw the graphs corresponding to relations such as $y = 3x - 1$, $2x + 3y = 6$, $y = x^2 - 2x - 1$, $y = 9 - x^2$ and $y = \frac{2}{x}$. If you are following the EXTENDED syllabus, you will be expected to draw graphs for other types of relations and to use the graphs to solve equations.

The methods are exactly the same as those you've learned in Unit 2. The tables of values may take a little longer to work out, partly because the algebraic expressions are more complicated and partly because you need to plot more points to be sure that you have the shape of the graph correct. In general, however, the work is reasonably straightforward and you should find it quite enjoyable.

This unit is divided into three sections:

Section	Title	Time
A	Cubic curves	3 hours
B	Other curves	1 hour
C	The gradient of a curve	2 hours

By the end of this unit, you should be able to:

- draw graphs of cubic functions
- construct tables of values and draw graphs for $y = x^n$ (for $n = -2, -1, 0, 1, 2, 3$) and for simple sums of these functions
- construct tables of values and draw graphs for $y = a^x$
- find the gradient of a curve.

A Cubic curves

Functions such as $y = x^3 + 2x - 3$, $y = 8 - x^3$ and $y = 2x^3 - 3x^2$ are called **cubic functions**. They are all of the form $y = ax^3 + bx^2 + cx + d$, where a, b, c, d are numbers. Notice that the highest power of x is x cubed. When we draw the graphs of these functions, we find that they are curves which have a family resemblance – they are all basically of the same shape. Their shape is different from that of a quadratic function (parabola) and different from that of a reciprocal function.

Example 1

Draw the graph of the function $y = x^3 - 6x$ for $-3 \leq x \leq 3$.

Solution

You must first work out a table of corresponding values of x and y.

x	-3	-2	-1	0	1	2	3
x^3	-27	-8	-1	0	1	8	27
$-6x$	$+18$	$+12$	$+6$	0	-6	-12	-18
$y = x^3 - 6x$	-9	$+4$	$+5$	0	-5	-4	$+9$

When I plot the seven points corresponding to these values of x and y, I find that I cannot be sure of the exact shape of the graph. This is because there is a big gap between some adjacent points and because the graph rises then falls, and then rises again, and I can't be sure where the 'top' and 'bottom' of the graph are.

So I've extended the table to include the 'half values' of x.

x	-2.5	-1.5	-0.5	$+0.5$	$+1.5$	$+2.5$
x^3	-15.625	-3.375	-0.125	$+0.125$	$+3.375$	$+15.625$
$-6x$	$+15$	$+9$	$+3$	-3	-9	-15
$y = x^3 - 6x$	-0.625	$+5.625$	$+2.875$	-2.875	-5.625	$+0.625$

I now can plot thirteen points on the graph. The shape of the graph is clearer now and, on the diagram below, I've joined them with a smooth curve.

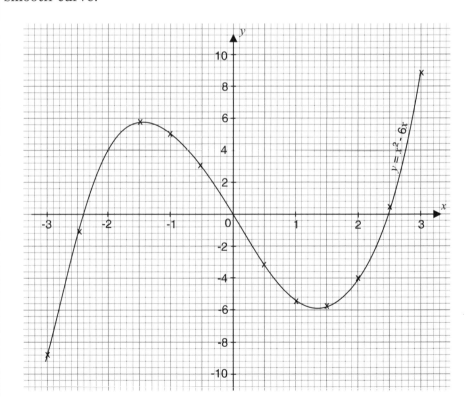

Example 2

Draw the graph of the function $y = x^3 - 2x^2 - 1$ for $-1 \leq x \leq 3$.
Use the graph to solve the equations:
a) $x^3 - 2x^2 - 1 = 0$
b) $x^3 - 2x^2 = -1$
c) $x^3 - 2x^2 - 5 = 0$

Solution

Taking into account our experience with Example 1, I will work out the values of y for whole number values of x and also the 'half values' of x.

x	-1	-0.5	0	0.5	1	1.5	2	2.5	3
x^3	-1	-0.125	0	0.125	1	3.375	8	15.625	27
$-2x^2$	-2	-0.5	0	-0.5	-2	-4.5	-8	-12.5	-18
-1	-1	-1	-1	-1	-1	-1	-1	-1	-1
$y = x^3 - 2x^2 - 1$	-4	-1.625	-1	-1.375	-2	-2.125	-1	$+2.125$	$+8$

The graph can now be drawn.

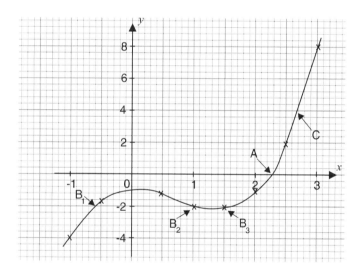

a) To solve the equation $x^3 - 2x^2 - 1 = 0$, I must find the point(s) on the curve which have a y-coordinate of 0. There is just one such point – it is labelled A. The x-coordinate of A is 2.2 and hence the solution of $x^3 - 2x^2 - 1 = 0$ is $x = 2.2$.

b) To solve the equation $x^3 - 2x^2 = -1$, I must first rearrange it so that the left-hand side is the function y. Subtracting 1 from both sides, the equation becomes $x^3 - 2x^2 - 1 = -2$. I have to find the point(s) on the curve which have a y-coordinate of -2. There are three such points – they are labelled B_1, B_2 and B_3. The x-coordinates of these points are the solutions of the equation. Hence, the solutions of $x^3 - 2x^2 = -1$ are $x = -0.6$, 1 and 1.6.

c) As in part b), I need to rearrange the equation $x^3 - 2x^2 - 5 = 0$ if I want to use the graph of $y = x^3 - 2x^2 - 1$ to solve it. Adding 4 to both sides of the equation, I get $x^3 - 2x^2 - 1 = 4$ and so I must find the point(s) on the curve which have a y-coordinate of 4.

There is only one such point (marked C on the diagram) and, from its x-coordinate, I deduce that the solution of the equation $x^3 - 2x^2 - 5 = 0$ is $x = 2.7$.

Example 3

Draw the graph of the function $y = 1 + 7x - x^3$ for $-3 \leq x \leq 3$.

Solution

The table of values is shown below. In this case, I have dealt with the whole number values of x first, and then the 'half values'.

x	-3	-2	-1	0	1	2	3
1	1	1	1	1	1	1	1
$+7x$	-21	-14	-7	0	$+7$	$+14$	$+21$
$-x^3$	$+27$	$+8$	$+1$	0	-1	-8	-27
$y = 1 + 7x - x^3$	$+7$	-5	-5	1	$+7$	$+7$	-5

x	-2.5	-1.5	-0.5	0.5	1.5	2.5
1	1	1	1	1	1	1
$+7x$	-17.5	-10.5	-3.5	$+3.5$	$+10.5$	$+17.5$
$-x^3$	$+15.625$	$+3.375$	$+0.125$	-0.125	-3.375	-15.625
$y = 1 + 7x - x^3$	-0.875	-6.125	-2.375	$+4.375$	$+8.125$	$+2.875$

The graph is shown below. Notice that, although this graph has the same shape as the graphs in Examples 1 and 2, it starts at top-left and finishes at bottom-right. In Examples 1 and 2, the graphs start at bottom-left and finish at top-right. Can you see how this is related to the coefficient of x^3 in the functions being graphed?

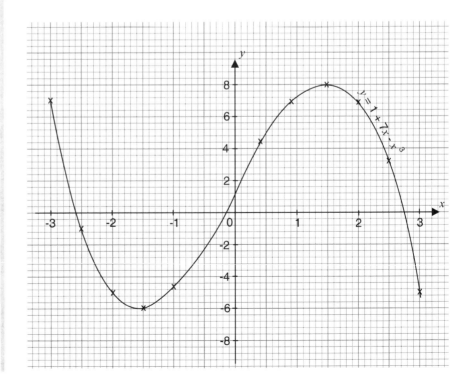

Example 4

On the same diagram, draw the graphs of the functions $y = x^3$ and $y = 2x - 1$ for $-2 \leq x \leq 2$. Hence solve the equation $x^3 = 2x - 1$.

Solution

The graph of $y = 2x - 1$ is a straight line so we will plot only three points to obtain it.

x	-2	0	2
$y = 2x - 1$	-5	-1	$+3$

The table of values for $y = x^3$ is shown below.

x	-2	-1.5	-1	-0.5	0	0.5	1	1.5	2
$y = x^3$	-8	-3.375	-1	-0.125	0	$+0.125$	$+1$	$+3.375$	$+8$

The graphs are shown in this diagram.

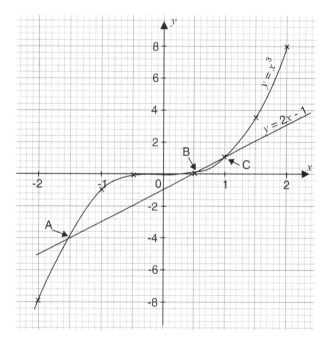

To solve the equation $x^3 = 2x - 1$, I have to find the value(s) of x for which the y-coordinate on the curve $y = x^3$ is equal to the y-coordinate on the line $y = 2x - 1$.

This means that I have to look for points which are common to the curve and the line.

From the diagram, I can see that there are three such points, A, B and C.

Their x-coordinates are the solutions. So, the solutions of the equation $x^3 = 2x - 1$ are $x = -1.6, 0.6, 1$.

It is now time for you to draw some cubic graphs. Remember that these graphs have a distinctive S shape.

The S could be quite pronounced, like this   or

but it could be quite shallow, like this   or

If the coefficient of x^3 is positive, then the graph is 'down at the left and up at the right'. If the coefficient of x^3 is negative, the graph is 'up at the left and down at the right'.

EXERCISE 11

1. a) Complete the table of values for the function $y = x^3 - 6x^2 + 8x$.

x	-1	-0.5	0	0.5	1	1.5	2	2.5	3	3.5	4	4.5	5
$y = x^3 - 6x^2 + 8x$	-15	-5.6		2.6		1.9		-1.9		-2.6		5.6	15

b) On the axes below, draw the graph of the function $y = x^3 - 6x^2 + 8x$ for $-1 \leq x \leq 5$.

c) Use the graph to solve the equations:
   (i) $x^3 - 6x^2 + 8x = 0$
   (ii) $x^3 - 6x^2 + 8x = 3$

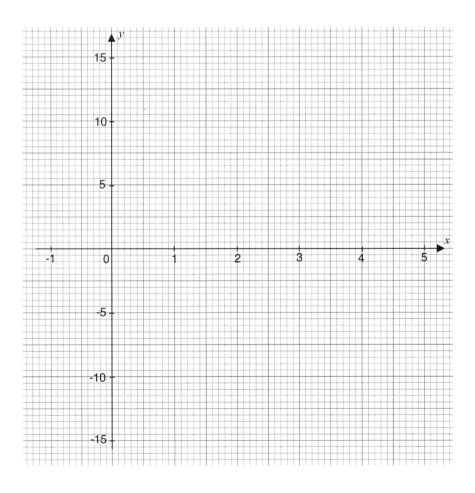

2. On the axes below, draw the graphs of $y = x^3 - 3x^2$ and $y = 3x - 2$. Hence solve the equation $x^3 - 3x^2 = 3x - 2$.

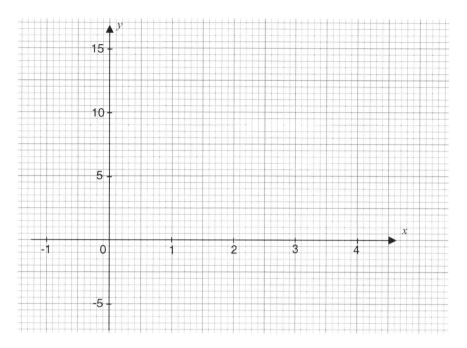

Check your answers at the end of this module.

B Other curves

In the IGCSE examination, you will be expected to be able to draw and use graphs for functions of the type $y = ax^n$ (where $n = -2, -1, 0, 1, 2$ or 3) and sums of such functions. This means graphs of functions such as
$$y = 2x^2 - x - 1, y = x^2 + \frac{36}{x} \text{ and } y = \frac{x^3}{12} - \frac{6}{x}.$$

There will never be more than three terms in these functions.

The last type of function you will have to deal with is $y = a^x$ (where a is a positive whole number). This is sometimes called the **growth function** or the **exponential function**. It is useful in describing mathematically any situation where the rate of increase of a quantity at any time is proportional to the size of the quantity at that time. This occurs, for example, in the growth of a population (human beings or animals).

Example 1

Draw the graph of the function $y = x^2 + \frac{36}{x}$ for $0.5 \leq x \leq 8$.

Use the graph to estimate the smallest possible value of $x^2 + \frac{36}{x}$ for values of x in the range $0.5 \leq x \leq 8$.

Solution

A table of corresponding values of x and y is shown below.

x	0.5	1	2	3	4	5	6	7	8
$y = x^2 + \frac{36}{x}$	72.25	37	22	21	25	32.2	42	54.1	68.5

The shape of the graph is clear. There is no need to plot more than 9 points.

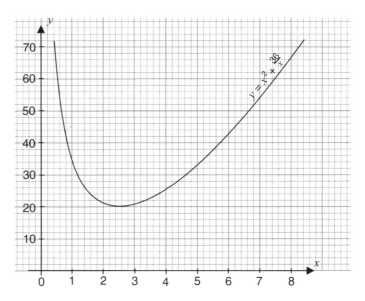

The lowest point on the curve will give us the smallest possible value of $x^2 + \frac{36}{x}$.

The lowest value of y is about 20.5 and the corresponding value of x is 2.6.

It follows that the smallest possible value of $x^2 + \frac{36}{x}$ for $0.5 \leq x \leq 8$ is 20.5.

> It is worth checking this by substituting $x = 2.6$ in $x^2 + \frac{36}{x}$. You will find that this gives 20.6.

Example 2

On the same axes, draw the graphs of $y = x + 10$ and $y = \frac{36}{x^2}$ for $-4 \leqslant x \leqslant 4$.

Use the graphs to find two solutions of the equation $\frac{36}{x^2} = x + 10$. Does this equation have more than two solutions?

Solution

The graph of $y = x + 10$ is a straight line. It passes through the points $(-4, 6)$, $(0, 10)$ and $(4, 14)$.

Remember that $\frac{36}{x^2}$ has no value when $x = 0$, so the graph of $y = \frac{36}{x^2}$ has a break in it at $x = 0$. A table of values is shown below.

x	-4	-3	-2	-1	0	1	2	3	4
$y = \frac{36}{x^2}$	$+2.25$	$+4$	$+9$	$+36$		$+36$	$+9$	$+4$	$+2.25$

It is worth calculating the value of y for $x = 1.5$. It is 16. The y-value for $x = -1.5$ is also 16.

The two graphs are shown here.

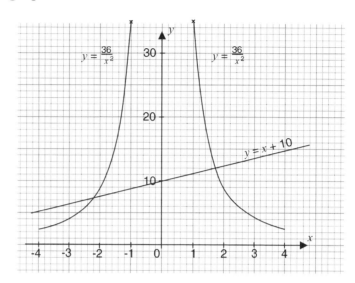

To find the solutions of the equation $\frac{36}{x^2} = x + 10$, I must read off the x-coordinates of the points where the graphs cross. The two solutions are $x = -2.2$ and $x = 1.7$.

I must now consider whether the graphs will cross again if they are extended outside the range $-4 \leq x \leq 4$.

It is clear that the value of $x + 10$ increases as x increases beyond $x = 4$, but the value of $\frac{36}{x^2}$ decreases. Hence, the graphs will not cross when $x > 4$.

At $x = -4$, the graph of $y = x + 10$ is above the curve $y = \frac{36}{x^2}$. The graph of $y = x + 10$ crosses the x-axis where $x = -10$, but $\frac{36}{x^2}$ is always

positive so the curve always stays above the x-axis. It follows that the graphs must cross at some point for which $x < -4$. Hence, the equation $\frac{36}{x^2} = x + 10$ has more than two solutions. [in fact it has three]

Example 3

Draw the graph of the function $y = 2^x$ for $-2 \leq x \leq 4$. Use your graph to find the value of $2^{2.5}$ and check your result by using the fact that $2^{2.5} = 2^{\frac{5}{2}} = \sqrt{2^5}$.

Solution

To work out the table of corresponding values of x and y, you need to remember the rules of indices from Module 2 Unit 3.
For example, $2^4 = 2 \times 2 \times 2 \times 2 = 16$
$2^0 = 1$
$2^{-1} = \frac{1}{2} = 0.5$
$2^{-2} = \frac{1}{2^2} = \frac{1}{4} = 0.25$

The table of values is as follows:

x	−2	−1	0	1	2	3	4
$y = 2^x$	0.25	0.5	1	2	4	8	16

From the graph, which is drawn below, we can see that, when $x = 2.5$, the value of y is 5.75.

We deduce that the value of $2^{2.5}$ is approximately 5.75.

Check: $2^{2.5} = 2^{\frac{5}{2}} = \sqrt{2^5} = \sqrt{32} = 5.66$.

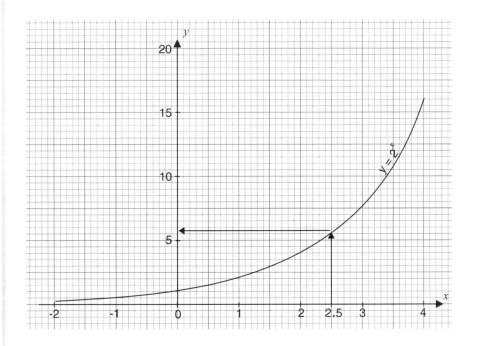

You should now be able to tackle the two questions in the next exercise.

EXERCISE 12

1. a) Complete this table of values for the function $y = 3x - \frac{12}{x}$.

x	1	1.5	2	2.5	3	3.5	4	4.5	5
$y = 3x - \frac{12}{x}$		−3.5	0		5	7.1		10.8	

   b) On the axes below, draw the graph of $y = 3x - \frac{12}{x}$ for $1 \leq x \leq 5$.

c) Use the graph to find the positive solution of the equation:
   (i) $3x - \frac{12}{x} = 10$
   (ii) $3x - \frac{12}{x} = -5$

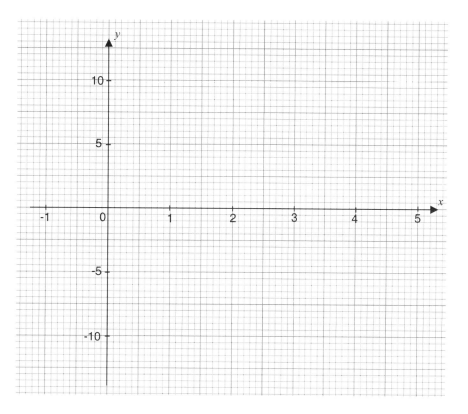

2.

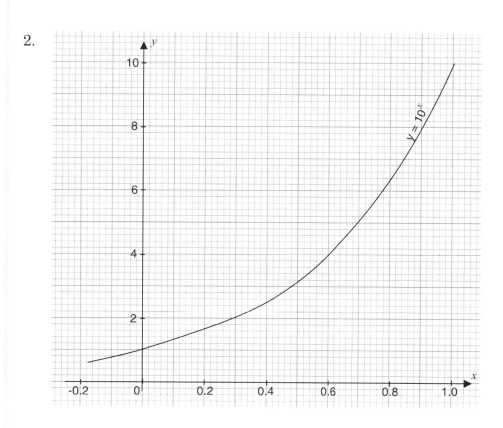

The graph of $y = 10^x$ for $-0.2 \leq x \leq 1.0$ is shown above.

a) Use the graph to find the value of:
   (i) $10^{0.3}$
   (ii) $10^{-0.1}$
b) In the diagram, draw a straight line graph which will enable you to solve the equation $10^x = 8 - 5x$.
   Write down the solution of this equation.

Check your answers at the end of this module.

C The gradient of a curve

Do you remember that, in Unit 2 Section A, you learnt how to calculate the gradient of a straight line graph? I now want to extend this idea and consider what is meant by 'the gradient of a curve'.

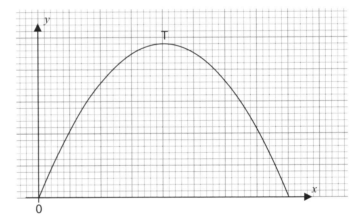

Look at this graph which represents the path of a cricket ball. The x-axis represents the horizontal ground and the y-axis represents the vertical line through the point 0 from which the ball was thrown. The path of the ball is quite steep at first but, by the time the ball reaches its highest point T, it is moving horizontally – the steepness has reduced to zero.

After the ball has passed the highest point, its path gets steeper and steeper in a downwards direction.

For a straight line graph, we defined the gradient to be the measure of its steepness. Since a straight line rises (or falls) at a constant rate, its gradient is constant. It is clear that the steepness of a curve is *not* constant and so we cannot talk about *the* gradient of a curve – the steepness (and therefore the gradient) changes from point to point.

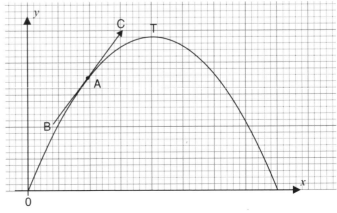

Consider the situation when the cricket ball is at the point A in the diagram. The direction in which the ball is travelling is shown by the line BAC. (If gravity suddenly ceased to exist, this is the direction in which the ball would move.) We shall define the gradient of the curve at the point A to be the gradient of the straight line BAC.

The line BAC just *touches* the curve at A – it does not cross it – and we say that it is the **tangent** to the curve at A.

We can now give the following definition:

> The gradient of a curve at a point is the gradient of the tangent to the curve at that point.

Drawing a tangent to a curve

When you find the gradient of a curve by drawing and measuring, the accuracy of your result depends on the accuracy of the curve you have drawn and the accuracy of the tangent you draw. It is particularly important that you position the tangent correctly.

Let A be the point at which you want to draw the tangent.

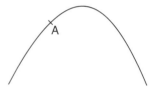

Turn the page round until A is the point on the curve nearest to you. Place your ruler below the curve and move it upwards until it touches the curve. If the point of contact is not A, rotate the ruler (so that it rolls along the curve) until the point of contact is A.

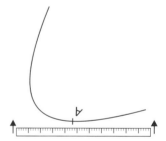

Use a pencil to draw the tangent.

There should be no gap between the tangent and the curve. The tangent must pass through A and not through any other point on the curve near A.

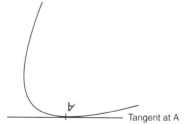

Tangent at A

Calculating the gradient of the tangent

1. If the tangent is rising from left to right, its gradient is positive. If the tangent is falling from left to right, its gradient is negative.
2. Remember that NQ and PN *must* be measured according to the scales on the y-axis and x-axis respectively. Failure to do this is the most common error made by examination candidates in calculating gradients.

Mark two points, P and Q, on the tangent. Try to make the horizontal distance between P and Q a whole number of units (measured on the x-axis scale).

Draw a horizontal line through P and a vertical line through Q to form a right-angled triangle PNQ.

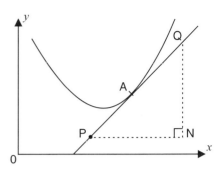

Gradient of the curve at A = Gradient of the tangent PAQ
$$= \frac{\text{distance NQ (measured on the } y\text{-axis scale)}}{\text{distance PN (measured on the } x\text{-axis scale)}}$$

Example 1

The graph of the function $y = 5x - x^2$ is shown in the diagram. Find the gradient of the graph:
  a) at the point (1, 4)
  b) at the point (3, 6)

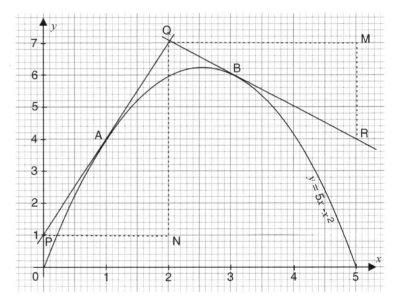

Solution

a) At the point A (1, 4), gradient $= \frac{\text{NQ}}{\text{PN}} = \frac{6}{2} = 3$.

b) At the point B (3, 6), gradient $= \frac{\text{MR}}{\text{QM}} = -\frac{3}{3} = -1$.

Example 2

The graph shows the height of a tree (y metres) plotted against the age of the tree (x years).
Estimate the rate at which the tree was growing when it was 4 years old.

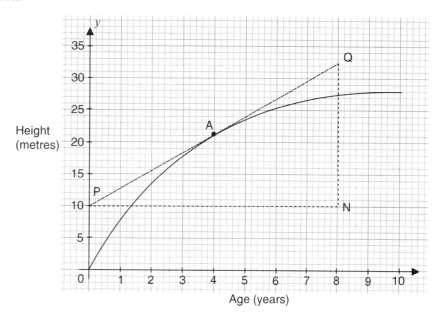

Solution

The rate at which the tree was growing when it was 4 years old is equal to the gradient of the curve at the point where $x = 4$.
The tangent at this point (A) has been drawn.

Gradient of the curve at A $= \dfrac{\text{NQ}}{\text{PN}} = \dfrac{22.5}{8} = 2.8$

The tree was growing at a rate of 2.8 metres per year.

Here are two questions for you to try.

EXERCISE 13

1. The graph of the function $y = x^2$ is shown in the diagram.
   a) Find the gradient of the graph at the point:
      (i) (2, 4)
      (ii) (−1, 1)

b) The gradient of the graph at the point (1.5, 2.25) is 3. Write down the coordinates of the point at which the gradient is −3.

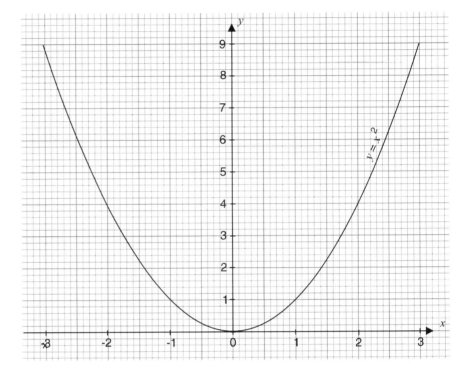

2. The graph shows how the population of a village has changed since 1930. Find the gradient of the graph at the point (1950, 170). What does this gradient represent?

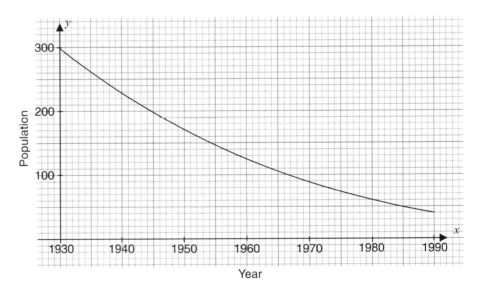

Check your answers at the end of this module.

Summary

In this unit you've practised drawing graphs by plotting points. You can see that as long as you calculate enough points to know what the curve will look like, you can draw cubic graphs, graphs for $y = x^n$ or graphs for $y = a^x$. You've also learnt how to calculate the gradient at a point on a curve, by calculating the gradient of the tangent at that point.

In the next unit you'll become familiar with function notation and I'll introduce you to some problems in linear programming.

Check your progress

1. Answer the whole of this question on the sheet of graph paper provided.

x	0.6	1	1.5	2	2.5	3	3.5	4	4.5	5
y	p	-5.9	-3.7	-2.3	-1.1	0.3	1.9	3.8	q	r

Some of the values for the function $y = \frac{x^3}{12} - \frac{6}{x}$ are shown in the table above.

Values of y are given correct to one decimal place.

a) Find the values of p, q and r.

b) Using a scale of 2cm to represent 1 unit on the x-axis, and 1 cm to represent 1 unit on the y-axis, draw the graph of $y = \frac{x^3}{12} - \frac{6}{x}$ for $0.6 \leq x \leq 5$.

c) Find, from your graph, correct to 1 decimal place, the value of x for which $\frac{x^3}{12} - \frac{6}{x} = 0$.

d) Draw the tangent to the curve at the point where $x = 1$, and hence estimate the gradient of the curve at that point.

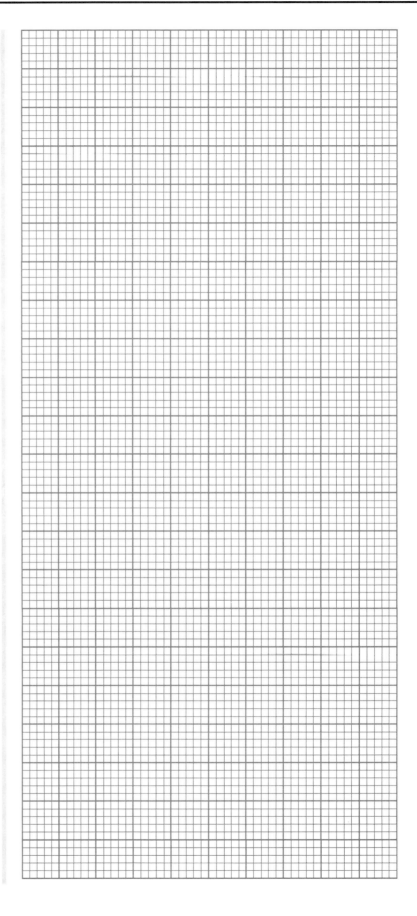

2. Look at the sketch graphs, I, II, III, IV, V, VI drawn below.
   a) Which one could be the graph of $y = 1 + x - 2x^2$?
   b) Which one could be the graph of $y = 3^x$?
   c) Which one could be the graph of $y = x^3 + x^2 + 1$?
   d) Which one could be the graph of $y = -\frac{16}{x^2}$?

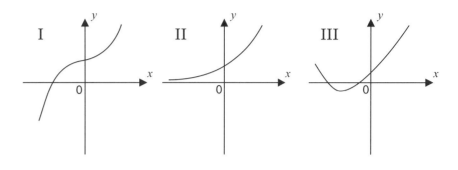

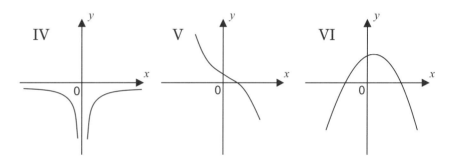

3. a) In a chemical reaction, the mass M grams of a chemical is given by the formula $M = 160 \times 2^{-t}$, where t is the time, in minutes, after the start.

   A table of values for t and M is given below.

t	0	1	2	3	4	5	6	7
M	p	80	40	20	q	5	r	1.25

   (i) Find the values of p, q and r.
   (ii) Draw the graph of M against t for $0 \leq t \leq 7$.
   Use a scale of 2 cm to represent 1 minute on the horizontal t-axis and 1cm to represent 10 grams on the vertical M-axis.
   (iii) Draw a suitable tangent to your graph and use it to estimate the rate of change of mass when $t = 2$.
   b) The other chemical in the same reaction has mass m grams which is given by $m = 160 - M$.
   For what value of t do the two chemicals have equal mass?

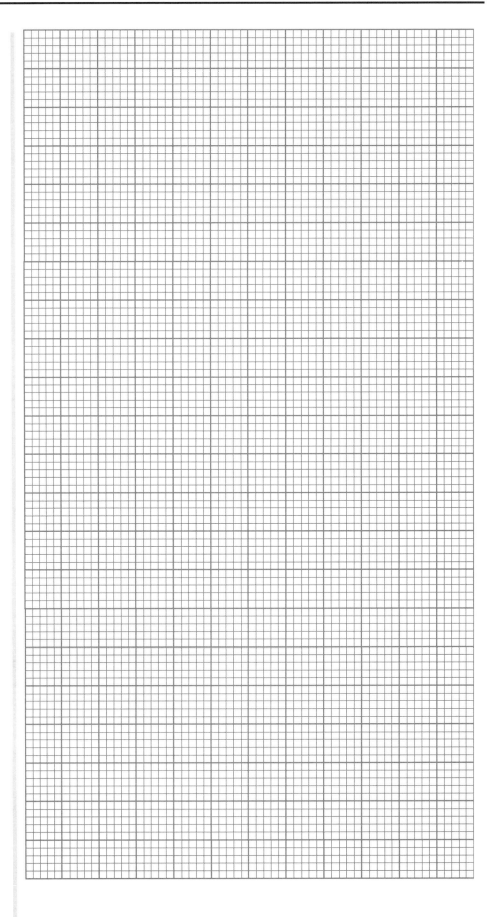

Check your answers at the end of this module.

Unit 4
Function Notation and Linear Programming

In the last unit in this module you'll be learning about functions and their inverses. Next up is some work explaining linear inequalities, to prepare you for the final section on linear programming.

This unit is divided into three sections:

Section	Title	Time
A	Functions	2 hours
B	Inequalities and regions in a plane	5 hours
C	Linear programming	5 hours

By the end of this unit, you should be able to:

- understand and use the notation $f(x) = 6 - 3x$ and the notation $f : x \mapsto 6 - 3x$ for functions
- evaluate compound functions
- find the inverse of a function and use the notation $f^{-1}(x)$
- represent graphically linear inequalities in two variables
- solve simple linear programming problems.

A Functions

If the value of a variable y depends on the value of another variable x in such a way that for each value of x, there is one and only one value of y, then y is said to be a **function** of x.

We have already met functions where the relationship between x and y can be expressed in algebraic form. The idea of a function is, however, much wider than this. For example, the symbol given to a candidate in an examination depends on the mark the candidate scores. Suppose the relationship is as shown in this table:

Mark scored	Symbol
85–100	A
65–84	B
50–64	C
40–49	D
0–39	U

The symbol is a function of the mark scored because, given the mark scored, you can determine which symbol will be given. There is one and only one symbol for each possible mark, e.g. a mark of 68 gets a symbol of B.

Notation for functions

Note, however, that the mark scored is *not* a function of the symbol because, given the symbol awarded to a candidate, there is more than one possible mark the candidate could have scored, e.g. a symbol of B could mean a mark of 65 or 66 or ... or 84.

Instead of using the letter y, it is common to use $f(x)$ to denote a function of x. This is read as 'f of x' and it must not be confused with f times x. The notation $f(x)$ emphasises that we are dealing with a *function* of x, rather than a more general relation between two variables. It is also a useful form of shorthand.

Consider the function $f(x) = 6 - 3x$. Then $f(5)$ means the value of the function when $x = 5$. $f(5) = 6 - 15 = -9$.
Similarly, $f(-2) = 6 - 3(-2) = 6 + 6 = 12$
and $f(0.5) = 6 - 3(0.5) = 6 - 1.5 = 4.5$

You will sometimes see a function written in a slightly different way. For example, $f(x) = 6 - 3x$ may be written as $f: x \mapsto 6 - 3x$. This would be read as 'f is the function which maps x onto $6 - 3x$'.

The number $6 - 3x$ is said to be the *image* of x under the function f. You need to understand this notation and be able to change from (for example) $f: x \mapsto x^3 + 4x - 1$ to $f(x) = x^3 + 4x - 1$, and vice versa, without any problem.

When there are two or more functions in the same problem it is necessary to use different symbols for them.
For example, $g(x) = x^2 - 2x - 3$ and $h(x) = 4x + 1$.
In this case, $g(2) = 4 - 4 - 3 = -3$ and $h(2) = 8 + 1 = 9$.

It is sometimes important to emphasise that a function is a sequence of operations. For example, given that $f: x \mapsto 2x + 3$, we can say that the function f is 'double and then add 3'.

With this in mind, you should realise that $x \mapsto 2x + 3$ and $t \mapsto 2t + 3$ are the same function, and they are the same as $y \mapsto 2y + 3$. (We say that the 'x' in $x \mapsto 2x + 3$ is a 'dummy variable' because it can be changed to any other letter without affecting the meaning.)

Example 1

Given the functions $f(x) = x^2 - 3x$ and $g(x) = 4x - 6$, find the value of:
a) $f(6)$
b) $f(-3)$
c) $g(\frac{1}{2})$
d) $g(6)$

Solution

a) $f(6) = 36 - 18 = 18$
b) $f(-3) = (-3)^2 - 3(-3) = 9 + 9 = 18$
c) $g(\frac{1}{2}) = 2 - 6 = -4$
d) $g(6) = 24 - 6 = 18$

Example 2

Given the function $h: x \mapsto 9 - x^2$, find the image of:

a)   0   b)   3   c)   9

Solution

The function can be written as $h(x) = 9 - x^2$.

a)   The image of $0 = h(0) = 9 - 0 = 9$.
b)   The image of $3 = h(3) = 9 - 9 = 0$.
c)   The image of $9 = h(9) = 9 - 81 = -72$.

Example 3

Given the functions $f(x) = x^2$ and $g(x) = x + 2$:

a)   solve the equation $f(x) = g(x)$
b)   solve the equation $4g(x) = g(x) - 3$

Solution

a) $f(x) = g(x)$ means that $x^2 = x + 2$
               This is $x^2 - x - 2 = 0$
                 $(x - 2)(x + 1) = 0$
       The solutions are $x = 2$ and $x = -1$
       Check: $f(2) = 2^2 = 4$ and $g(2) = 2 + 2 = 4$ } The solution
              $f(-1) = (-1)^2 = 1$ and $g(-1) = (-1) + 2 = 1$ is checked.

b) $4g(x) = g(x) - 3$ means that $3g(x) = -3$ and so $g(x) = -1$
          Hence $x + 2 = -1$
          and $x = -3$
   Check: $g(-3) = (-3) + 2 = -1$
             Hence $4g(-3) = -4$ and $g(-3) - 3 = -1 - 3 = -4$
             so $4g(-3) = g(-3) - 3$. The solution is checked.

Test your understanding of the notation by doing a few questions.

EXERCISE 14

1. Given the functions $f(x) = x^3 - 8$ and $g(x) = 3 - x$, find the values of:

    a) $f(2)$
    b) $f(-1)$
    c) $g(5)$
    d) $g(-2)$

2. Given the function $h: x \mapsto 4x^2$, find the image of:

    a)   2
    b) -2
    c) $\frac{1}{2}$

3. Given the functions $f(x) = x^2 - x$ and $g(x) = x^2 + 3x - 12$:

    a)   solve the equation $f(x) = 6$
    b)   solve the equation $f(x) = g(x)$

4. $f(x) = \dfrac{4+x}{x}$ $(x \neq 0)$
   a) Calculate $f(\tfrac{1}{2})$, simplifying your answer.
   b) Solve $f(x) = 3$.

Check your answers at the end of this module.

Composite functions

A composite function is sometimes called a 'function of a function' – it is the result of applying one function to a number and then applying another function to the result. Some examples will make this clear.

Consider the two functions $f(x) = 2x + 1$ and $g(x) = x^2$.

If we apply the function f to the number 4, we get $f(4) = 9$.
We now apply the function g to the number 9 and we get $g(9) = 81$.

This would be written as $g[f(4)] = 81$.

Notice that, if we apply function g first and function f second, we get a different result: $g(4) = 4^2 = 16$
$$f(16) = 32 + 1 = 33$$
and so $f[g(4)] = 33$

These two results would usually be shortened to
$gf(4) = 81$ and $fg(4) = 33$.

It is important that you remember that

$$gf(x) \text{ stands for } g[f(x)]$$

$gf(x)$ is a composite function in which f is applied first and g second.

Example

Given the functions $f(x) = x^2 - 2x$ and $g(x) = 3 - x$, find the values of:
a) $gf(4)$
b) $fg(4)$
c) $ff(-1)$
d) $gg(100)$

Solution

a) $gf(4) = g[f(4)] = g[16 - 8] = g[8] = 3 - 8 = -5$
b) $fg(4) = f[g(4)] = f[3 - 4] = f[-1] = (-1)^2 - 2(-1) = 1 + 2 = 3$
c) $ff(-1) = f[f(-1)] = f[1 + 2] = f[3] = 9 - 6 = 3$
d) $gg(100) = g[g(100)] = g[3 - 100] = g[-97]$
   $= 3 - (-97) = 3 + 97 = 100$

Here is a similar question for you to try.

EXERCISE 15

Given the functions $g(x) = x^2 + 1$ and $h(x) = 2x + 3$, find the values of:
a) $gh(1)$
b) $hg(1)$
c) $gg(2)$
d) $hh(5)$

Check your answers at the end of this module.

Flow diagrams

The steps to be taken to work out the value of a function $f(x)$ for any value of x can be shown in a flow diagram.

For example, for the function $f(x) = 2x + 5$, the steps are 'double' and 'add 5' (in that order). The flow diagram is as follows:

$$x \longrightarrow \boxed{\times 2} \xrightarrow{2x} \boxed{+ 5} \longrightarrow 2x + 5$$

For the function $g(x) = 2(x + 5)$, the steps are 'add 5' and 'double' (in that order) and the flow diagram is:

$$x \longrightarrow \boxed{+ 5} \xrightarrow{x+5} \boxed{\times 2} \longrightarrow 2(x + 5)$$

Notice that these two flow diagrams contain the same 'operation boxes' but the diagrams are different because the boxes are not in the same order.

Inverse of a function

The inverse of a function is the function which will 'do the opposite of f' or, in other words, will 'undo' the effects of f. For example, if f maps the number 4 onto the number 13, then the inverse of f will map the number 13 onto the number 4.

In general, if f is applied to a number and then the inverse of f is applied to that answer, you get back to the number you started with.

In simple cases, the inverse of a function can be found by common sense or, as a mathematician would say, 'by inspection'. For example, the inverse of $x \mapsto x + 5$ is $x \mapsto x - 5$ because to undo 'add 5', we must 'subtract 5'.

Similarly, the inverse of $x \mapsto 2x$ is $x \mapsto \frac{x}{2}$ because to undo 'multiply by 2' we must 'divide by 2'.

> The inverse of the function f is denoted by f^{-1}.

Hence, if $f(x) = x + 5$, then $f^{-1}(x) = x - 5$
and if $g(x) = 2x$, then $g^{-1}(x) = \frac{x}{2}$.

Not all functions have an inverse *function*.

For example, $x \mapsto x^2$ is a function because, for every value of x there is one and only one value of x^2. However, its inverse is not a function. The inverse of 'square' is 'take the square root', but a positive number has two square roots (one positive and one negative).

Finding the inverse of a function

Method 1 In this method, the flow diagram for the function is drawn and then the flow diagram for the inverse is obtained by reversing the flow and 'undoing' the operations in the boxes.

Example 1

Find the inverse of the function $f(x) = 3x - 4$.

Solution

The flow diagram for f is as follows:

Input $\rightarrow$ $\boxed{\times 3}$ $\rightarrow$ $\boxed{-4}$ $\rightarrow$ Output

The reversed flow diagram is

Output $\leftarrow$ $\boxed{\div 3}$ $\leftarrow$ $\boxed{+4}$ $\leftarrow$ Input

Writing x for the input in the reversed flow diagram, we obtain

$\frac{x+4}{3}$ $\leftarrow$ $\boxed{\div 3}$ $\overset{x+4}{\leftarrow}$ $\boxed{+4}$ $\leftarrow$ x

Hence, $f^{-1}(x) = \frac{x+4}{3}$

Check: Take $x = 10$. Then $f(10) = 30 - 4 = 26$

and $f^{-1}(26) = \frac{26+4}{3} = \frac{30}{3} = 10$ which is the number we started with.

Example 2

Given that $g(x) = 5 - 2x$, find $g^{-1}(x)$.

Solution

We take $g(x)$ as $-2x + 5$ and its flow diagram is

Input $\rightarrow$ $\boxed{\times -2}$ $\rightarrow$ $\boxed{+5}$ $\rightarrow$ Output

The reversed flow diagram is

Output $\leftarrow$ $\boxed{\div -2}$ $\leftarrow$ $\boxed{-5}$ $\leftarrow$ Input

Writing x for the input in the reversed flow diagram, we obtain

$\frac{x-5}{(-2)}$ $\leftarrow$ $\boxed{\div -2}$ $\overset{x+4}{\leftarrow}$ $\boxed{-5}$ $\leftarrow$ x

Hence, $g^{-1}(x) = \frac{x-5}{(-2)}$ which simplifies to $g^{-1}(x) = \frac{5-x}{2}$

Check: Take $x = 3$. Then $g(3) = 5 - 6 = -1$

and $g^{-1}(-1) = \frac{5-(-1)}{2} = \frac{6}{2} = 3$ which is the number we started with.

Method 2 In this method, we use the fact that, if f maps x onto y, then f^{-1} maps y onto x.

To find f^{-1} we have to find the value of x that corresponds to a given value of y. In other words, we have to rearrange the formula $y = $ expression in x into $x = $ expression in y.

Example 1

Find the inverse of the function $f(x) = 3x - 4$.

Solution

Suppose f maps x onto y. Then $y = 3x - 4$.
Make x the subject of the formula: $y + 4 = 3x$

$$\text{Hence } \frac{y + 4}{3} = x$$

Now f^{-1} maps y onto x and so $f^{-1}: y \mapsto \frac{y+4}{3}$

This means that $f^{-1}(y) = \frac{y+4}{3}$

As we mentioned on page 84, the 'y' in this formula is a 'dummy variable' and it can be replaced by any other letter, including x. Thus, we can say that, if $f(x) = 3x - 4$, then $f^{-1}(x) = \frac{x+4}{3}$.

Example 2

Given that $g(x) = 5 - 2x$, find $g^{-1}(x)$.

Solution

Let $y = 5 - 2x$, so we can say that g maps x onto y.
Make x the subject of the formula: $2x = 5 - y$

$$\text{and so } x = \frac{5-y}{2}$$

g^{-1} maps y onto x and hence $g^{-1}(y) = \frac{5-y}{2}$

$$\text{It follows that } g^{-1}(x) = \frac{5-x}{2}$$

Example 3

Given the function $h(x) = 3(x + 2)$, find the value of:
a) $h^{-1}(12)$ b) $h^{-1}h(4)$ c) $h^{-1}h^{-1}(33)$

Solution

Let $y = 3(x + 2)$, so we can say that h maps x onto y.
Make x the subject of the formula: $y = 3x + 6$
$$y - 6 = 3x$$
$$\frac{y-6}{3} = x$$

h^{-1} maps y onto x and hence $h^{-1}(y) = \frac{y-6}{3}$.

(To work out the values required in this question, we have no real need to change this to $h^{-1}(x) = \frac{x-6}{3}$.)

a) $h^{-1}(12) = \frac{12-6}{3} = \frac{6}{3} = 2$

b) $h^{-1}h(4) = h^{-1}[h(4)] = h^{-1}[18] = \frac{18-6}{3} = 4$

   (The result here should be obvious since h^{-1} undoes the effect of h.)

c) $h^{-1}h^{-1}(33) = h^{-1}[h^{-1}(33)] = h^{-1}[\frac{33-6}{3}] = h^{-1}[9] = \frac{9-6}{3} = 1$

For the questions in Exercise 16, you may use one or both of the two methods I have shown you for finding the inverse of a function. Find out which is the easier method for you and then use that method in all similar questions.

EXERCISE 16

1. Find the inverse of the function $f(x) = 4x + 3$.
2. Given the function $g(x) = \frac{x}{3} - 4$, find $g^{-1}(x)$.
3. Given the function $h(x) = 2(x - 3)$, find the value of:
   a) $h^{-1}(10)$ b) $hh^{-1}(20)$ c) $h^{-1}h^{-1}(26)$

Check your answers at the end of this module.

B Inequalities and regions in a plane

In this diagram, the 'broken' line is parallel to the x-axis. Every point on the line has a y-coordinate of 3. This means (as you know already) that the equation of the line is $y = 3$.

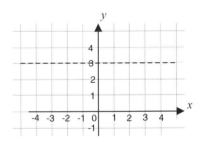

Consider now the points which are in the region above the line. Every point in the region has a y-coordinate greater than 3, and every point with a y-coordinate greater than 3 is in the region. We can say, therefore, that the region above the line represents the **inequality** $y > 3$. Similarly, the region below the line represents the inequality $y < 3$.

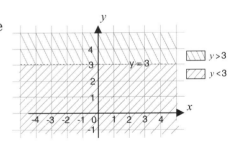

The graph of $y = 2x + 1$ is shown as a broken line in this diagram. Every point on the line has coordinates (x, y) which satisfy $y = 2x + 1$.

Consider a point P in the region above the line. You can see that its y-coordinate is greater than the y-coordinate of Q which is the point on the line vertically below P.

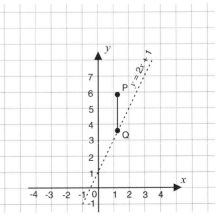

P and Q have the same x-coordinate and, for Q, $y = 2x + 1$. It follows that, for any point P in the region above the line, $y > 2x + 1$.

The region above the
line $y = 2x + 1$
represents the
inequality $y > 2x + 1$.

Similarly, the region below
the line represents the
inequality $y < 2x + 1$.

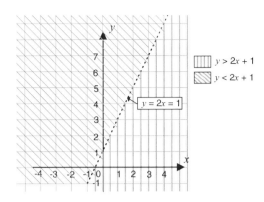

In the two examples above, the equations of the lines were in the
form $y = mx + c$. As a consequence,
   the inequality $y > mx + c$ was the region *above* the line.
and the inequality $y < mx + c$ was the region *below* the line.

If the equation of the line is not in the form $y = mx + c$, you have to
be careful when deciding which region represents which inequality.
You could change the subject of the formula so that the equation of
the line is in the form $y = mx + c$. But it is usually easier to consider
a 'check point', as illustrated in the following example.

Example

In a diagram, show the regions which represent the inequalities
   $2x - 3y < 6$ and $2x - 3y > 6$.

Solution

The boundary between the two
required regions is the
line $2x - 3y = 6$.

This line crosses the x-axis
at $(3, 0)$ and the y-axis at $(0, -2)$.
It is shown as a broken line
in this diagram.

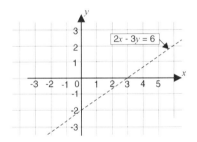

Consider any point in
the region above the line.
The easiest point to use is
the origin $(0, 0)$. When $x = 0$
and $y = 0$, $2x - 3y = 0$.
Since 0 is less than 6, the
region above the line
represents the
inequality $2x - 3y < 6$.

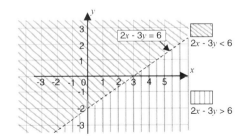

Hence, the region below the line must represent $2x - 3y > 6$. (Alternatively, you could consider a point in the region below the line, for example (4, 0). When $x = 4$ and $y = 0$, $2x - 3y = 8$. Since 8 is greater than 6, the region below the line represents the inequality $2x - 3y > 6$.)

Rules about boundaries and shading of regions

The inequalities which we want to represent graphically are not always *greater than* ($>$) or *less than* ($<$), they are often *greater than or equal to* ($\geq$), or *less than or equal to* ($\leq$).

Our graphical representations must show a difference between
greater than and *greater than or equal to*
and between *less than* and *less than or equal to*.

When the inequality includes *equal to*, the boundary line must be included in the graphical representation. It is, therefore, shown as a solid line. When the inequality does not include *equal to*, the boundary line is not included in the graphical representation and it is shown as a broken line.

To show which region represents a given inequality, there is more than one method available. For the IGCSE examination, the method you must use is to shade the region which is *not* required. (Think of this as 'crossing out' the unwanted region.) As you will see later, this is the most useful method for dealing with linear programming problems.

Example 1

By shading the unwanted region, show the region which represents the inequality $3x - 5y \leq 15$.

Solution

The boundary line is $3x - 5y = 15$ and it is included in the region (because the inequality includes *equal to*).

This line crosses the x-axis at (5, 0) and crosses the y-axis at (0, -3). It is shown as a solid line in this diagram.

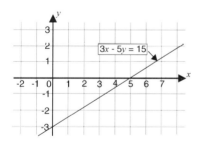

When $x = 0$ and $y = 0$, $3x - 5y = 0$. Since 0 is less than 15, the origin (0, 0) is in the required region. (Alternatively, re-arrange $3x - 5y \leq 15$ to get $y \geq \frac{3}{5}x - 3$ and deduce that the required region is *above* the line.)

The unshaded region in this diagram represents the inequality $3x - 5y \leq 15$.

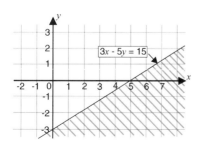

Example 2

By shading the unwanted region, show the region which represents the inequality $x + 2y > 6$.

Solution

The boundary line is $x + 2y = 6$ and it is *not* included in the region (because the inequality does not include 'equal to').

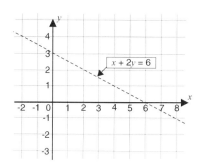

The line crosses the x-axis at (6, 0) and crosses the y-axis at (0, 3). It is shown as a broken line in this diagram.

When $x = 0$ and $y = 0$, $x + 2y = 0$. Since 0 is less than 6, the origin (0, 0) is *not* in the required region.

The unshaded region in this diagram represents the inequality $x + 2y > 6$.

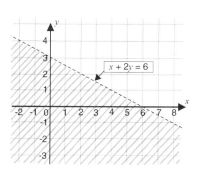

Example 3

By shading the unwanted region, show the region which represents the inequality $3x - 2y \geq 0$.

Solution

The boundary line is $3x - 2y = 0$ and it is included in the region. It is shown as a solid line in this diagram.

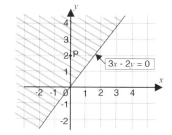

We cannot take the origin as the check-point because it lies on the boundary line. I'll take, instead, the point P (0, 2) which is above the line. When $x = 0$ and $y = 2$, $3x - 2y = -4$ which is less than 0. Hence P is *not* in the required region.

The unshaded region in this diagram represents the inequality $3x - 2y \geq 0$.

Example 4

Find the inequality which is represented by the unshaded region in this diagram.

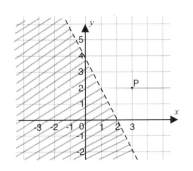

Solution

First find the equation of the boundary. Its gradient $= -\frac{4}{2} = -2$ and its intercept on the y-axis $= 4$. Hence the boundary line is $y = -2x + 4$, that is $y + 2x = 4$. Take P $(3, 2)$ as the check-point: $2 + 6 = 8$.

8 is greater than 4. Hence, the unshaded region represents $y + 2x > 4$. ⎡ no '=' because boundary is not included ⎤

Before we go on to consider simultaneous inequalities, you should try a few questions for yourself.

EXERCISE 17

1. By shading the unwanted region, show the region which represents the inequality $2y - 3x \geq 6$.

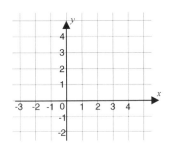

2. By shading the unwanted region, show the region which represents the inequality $x + 2y < 4$.

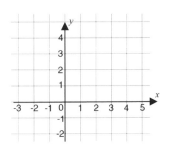

3. By shading the unwanted region, show the region which represents the inequality $x - y \geq 0$.

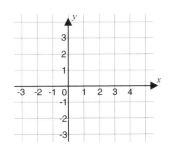

4. For each of the following diagrams, find the inequality which is represented by the unshaded region.

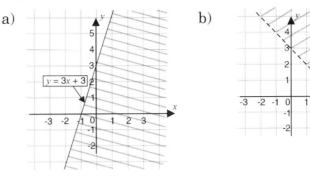

Check your answers at the end of this module.

Representing simultaneous inequalities

In practical problems, we usually find that we have to deal with two or more inequalities which have to be satisfied, all at the same time. You will remember learning how to deal with simultaneous equations – we will now consider **simultaneous inequalities**.

The method is a simple extension of the work you have just done. To find the values of x and y which satisfy several inequalities simultaneously, you represent the inequalities by regions on the same diagram, shading (or 'crossing-out') the unwanted regions. In the completed diagram, the unshaded region contains the points whose coordinates (x, y) satisfy all the inequalities simultaneously.

Example 1

By shading the unwanted regions, show the region defined by the set of inequalities $3x + 2y \geq 6$, $2x - 3y > 6$, $x \leq 4$.

Solution

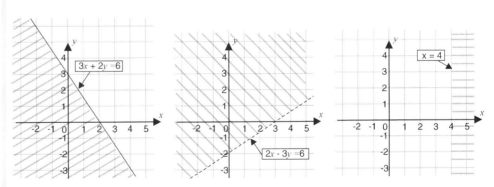

In the diagrams above, the unshaded regions represent the inequalities $3x + 2y \geq 6$, $2x - 3y > 6$ and $x \leq 4$ respectively.

Putting these regions on the same diagram, we obtain the diagram on the following page. The unshaded triangular region in this diagram is defined by the set of inequalities $3x + 2y \geq 6$, $2x - 3y > 6$, $x \leq 4$.

Note: The separate diagrams on the previous page have been drawn to make the method clear. When you answer questions of this type, you need only draw one diagram, similar to the one shown below.

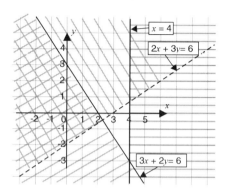

Example 2

By shading the unwanted regions, show the region which contains the points whose coordinates (x, y) satisfy all the inequalities $-2 \leq x \leq 3$, $y > x$, $y < 4$.

Solution

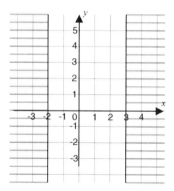
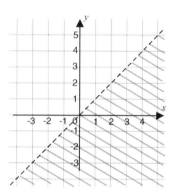

In the diagrams above and right, the unshaded regions represent the inequalities $-2 \leq x \leq 3$, $y > x$ and $y < 4$ respectively.

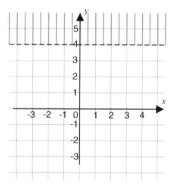

Putting these regions on the same diagram, we obtain this diagram. The unshaded region contains all the points whose coordinates (x, y) satisfy $-2 \leq x \leq 3$, $y > x$ and $y < 4$ simultaneously.

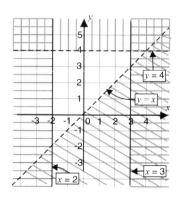

Example 3

Given that x and y are whole numbers, find the pairs of values (x, y) which satisfy all the inequalities $x + y \leq 4$, $y - 2x \leq 2$, $y > 0$.

Solution

The unshaded region in Diagram 1 represents the set of inequalities $x + y \leq 4$, $y - 2x \leq 2$, $y > 0$.

We now have to use the fact that, in this question, x and y have to be whole numbers. This means that the only points in the unshaded region that we need are the grid points. These are marked by dots in Diagram 2.

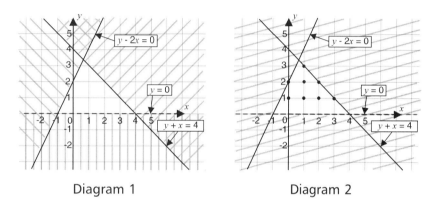

Diagram 1   Diagram 2

Using Diagram 2, we see that the pairs of whole numbers (x, y) which satisfy $x + y \leq 4$, $y - 2x \leq 2$ and $y > 0$ simultaneously are $(0, 1)$, $(0, 2)$, $(1, 1)$, $(1, 2)$, $(1, 3)$, $(2, 1)$, $(2, 2)$ and $(3, 1)$.

> remember that points on the broken line are *not* in the region

Example 4

By shading the unwanted regions, show the region defined by the set of inequalities $y < x + 2$, $y \leq 4$, $x \leq 3$.

Solution

The boundaries of the required region are $y = x + 2$ (broken line), $y = 4$ (solid line) and $x = 3$ (solid line).

The unshaded region in the diagram below represents the set of inequalities $y < x + 2$, $y \leq 4$, $x \leq 3$.

(Notice that this region does not have a finite area – it is not 'closed'.)

If you have followed the examples carefully, you should feel confident that you can do some questions for yourself. Do the following exercise.

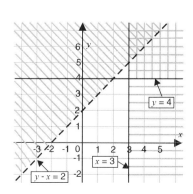

EXERCISE 18

1. By shading the unwanted regions, show the region defined by the set of inequalities $x + 2y \geq 6$, $y \leq x$, $x < 4$.

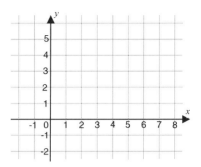

2. By shading the unwanted regions, show the region defined by the set of inequalities $x + y \geq 5$, $y \leq 2$, $y \geq 0$.

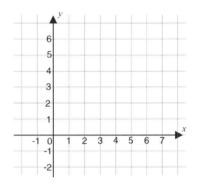

3. a) On the grid, draw the lines $x = 4$, $y = 3$ and $x + y = 5$.
   b) By shading the unwanted regions, show the region which satisfies all the inequalities $x \leq 4$, $y \leq 3$ and $x + y \geq 5$. Label the region R.

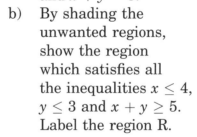

4. Write down the three inequalities which define the unshaded triangular region R in this diagram.

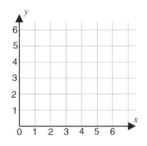

5. The unshaded region in the diagram below represents the set of inequalities $y \geq 0$, $y + 2x \geq 2$, $x + y < 4$. Write down the pairs of integers (x, y) which satisfy all the inequalities.

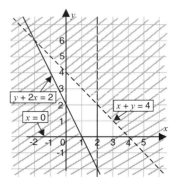

Check your answers at the end of this module.

C Linear programming

Many of the applications of mathematics in business and industry are concerned with obtaining the greatest profit or incurring the least cost, subject to restrictions such as the number of workers and machines available or the capital available.

Expressed in mathematical language, the restrictions take the form of inequalities and, when these inequalities are linear (such as $3x + 2y < 6$, which can be represented by a region with a straight line boundary), the branch of mathematics used is called **linear programming**.

Greatest and least values

Consider the expression $2x + y$.
This expression has a value at every point (x, y) in the cartesian plane. For example, at the point $(3, 1)$, $2x + y = 7$, at the point $(-2, 2)$, $2x + y = -2$.

Values of $2x + y$ at some grid points are shown in this diagram.

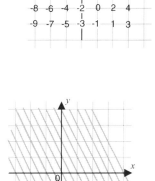

If we join points which give the same value of $2x + y$, we obtain a set of 'contour lines'. It should not surprise you that the contours are straight lines – their equations are of the form $2x + y =$ constant (k).

You can see that, as k increases, the line $2x + y = k$ moves parallel to itself towards the top right-hand side of the diagram. As k decreases, the line moves parallel to itself towards the bottom left-hand side of the diagram.

The expression $2x + y$ has no greatest or least value if there are no restrictions on the values of x and y. The value of the expression can be as large as you like, and it can be large positive or large negative.

When there are restrictions on the values of x and y, we shall find that there are restrictions on the value of expressions such as $2x + y$. There will usually be a greatest value and/or a least value.

Example 1

The numbers x and y satisfy all the inequalities
$x + y \leq 4$, $y \leq 2x - 2$ and $y \geq x - 2$.
Find the greatest and least possible values of the expression $2x + y$.

Solution

The unshaded triangular region in this diagram consists of the points (x, y) which satisfy all the inequalities $x + y \leq 4$, $y \leq 2x - 2$, $y \geq x - 2$.

notice that all three boundaries are included in the region

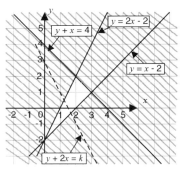

We have to consider the values of $2x + y$ for points in the unshaded region. If $2x + y = k$ then $y = -2x + k$. Draw a line with gradient $= -2$. Moving the line $2x + y = k$ parallel to itself towards the top right of the diagram, the value of k increases. The line is about to lose contact with the region when it passes through the point $(3, 1)$.

use your pencil to do this – put your pencil on the line $2x + y = k$ and then move it parallel to the line

$2x + y$ has its greatest value at this point. Hence, the greatest possible value of $2x + y$ is 7. Moving the line $2x + y = k$ towards the bottom left of the diagram, the value of k decreases. The line is about to lose contact with the region when it passes through the point $(0, -2)$. $2x + y$ has its least value at this point. Hence, the least possible value of $2x + y$ is -2.

substitute $x = 3$ and $y = 1$ into $2x + y$

substitute $x = 0$ and $y = -2$ into $2x + y$

Example 2

The numbers x and y satisfy all the inequalities
$x \geq 0$, $x + 2y \geq 7$, $2x + y \leq 8$ and $7x + 6y \leq 42$.
Find the greatest and least possible values of the expression $3x + 2y$.

Solution

The unshaded region ABCD in the diagram below consists of the points (x, y) which satisfy all the given inequalities.

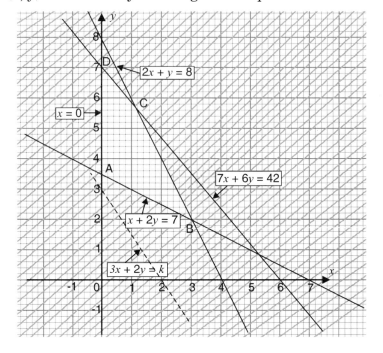

Consider the line $3x + 2y = k$. Find the gradient by making y the subject of the formula. $y = -\frac{3}{2}x + \frac{k}{2}$. The gradient is $-\frac{3}{2}$ so draw a line with this gradient anywhere on the cartesian plane. If we move this line parallel to itself towards the top right of the diagram, it will first come into contact with the region at the point A(0, 3.5). If we continue to move the line parallel to itself, its last point of contact with the region is the point C(1.2, 5.6).

It follows that the least possible value of $3x + 2y = 0 + 7 = 7$ and the greatest possible value of $3x + 2y = 3.6 + 11.2 = 14.8$.

In Examples 1 and 2, the greatest and least values of the given expression occurred at vertices of the region representing the inequalities. The reason for this is obvious when you consider the moving 'contour line'.

This gives another method of finding greatest and least values – work out the value of the expression at each of the vertices of the region and pick out the greatest and least of these values. However, if x and y have to be whole numbers (they may be a number of workers or a number of machines), the greatest and least values may not occur *at* vertices of the region representing the inequalities, although they will usually occur at grid points near vertices.

Example 3

The whole numbers x and y satisfy all the inequalities $x \geq 0$, $x + 2y \geq 7$, $2x + y \leq 8$, $7x + 6y \leq 42$.

Find the greatest and least possible values of the expression $3x + 2y$.

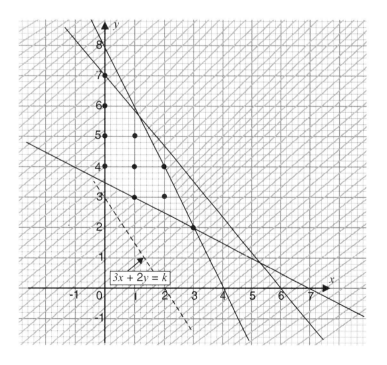

Solution

Notice that this is exactly the same as Example 2, except that, in this example, x and y have to be whole numbers. The unshaded region is obtained, as in Example 2, but the only points which are relevant are those with whole number coordinates – the grid points. There are 10 grid points in the region, as shown in the diagram. Considering the line $3x + 2y = k$ being moved parallel to itself, towards the top right of the diagram, it first comes into contact with the relevant grid points at $(0, 4)$. If we continue to move the line, its last points of contact are $(0, 7)$ and $(2, 4)$. It follows that the least possible value of $3x + 2y = 0 + 8 = 8$ and the greatest possible value of $3x + 2y = 0 + 14 = 14$ (or $6 + 8 = 14$).

Have you understood the work on greatest and least values? Here are some questions to test your understanding.

EXERCISE 19

1. In the diagram, the unshaded region represents the set of inequalities $x \leq 6$, $0 \leq y \leq 6$, $x + y \geq 4$.

   Find the greatest and least possible values of $3x + 2y$ subject to these inequalities.

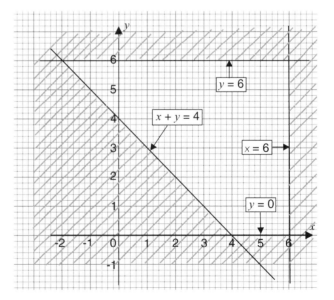

2. a) On the grid, indicate by shading the unwanted regions, the region satisfying all the inequalities
$y \leq x, x + y \leq 6, y \geq 0$.

b) What is the greatest possible value of $2x + y$ if x and y satisfy all these inequalities?

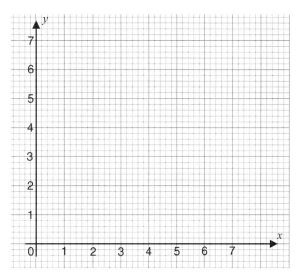

3. The whole numbers x and y satisfy all the inequalities $y \geq 1, y \leq x + 3$ and $3x + y \leq 6$.

Find the greatest and least possible values of the expression $x + y$.

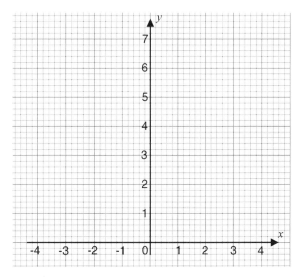

Check your answers at the end of this module.

Practical problems

Let's look at some practical applications.

The linear programming problems that occur in practice are usually so complicated that computers have to be used to solve them. However, it is worthwhile to look at some simplified problems to see how the work we have done on inequalities and greatest and least values can be used. In all cases, it is necessary to translate the problem into mathematical symbols – the conditions will translate into inequalities, and the quantity whose greatest or least value is required will translate into an expression containing x and y.

Example 1

A farmer keeps x cows and y sheep, where $x \geq 4$ and $y \geq 10$.

a) On graph paper, draw axes from 0 to 60, using a scale of 2 cm to represent 10 units on each axis.
    Draw and label the lines $x = 4$ and $y = 10$.
b) The total number of cows and sheep must not be more than 49. Write this as an inequality and draw the appropriate line on your graph.
c) Shade the *unwanted* regions of your graph.
d) The farmer makes R100 profit per cow and R50 per sheep. What is his maximum profit?

Solution

a) On the graph paper below, the lines $x = 4$ and $y = 10$ have been drawn.
b) The inequality is $x + y \leq 49$.
    The line $x + y = 49$ has been drawn on the graph paper.

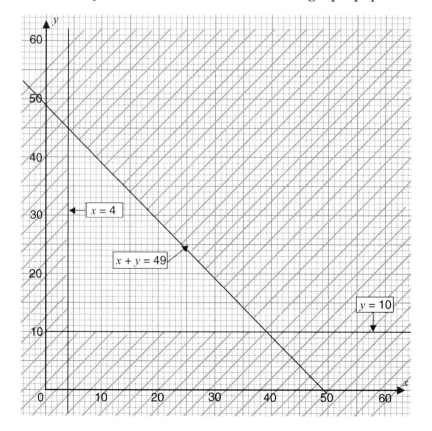

c) The unwanted regions are shaded on the graph paper.
d) The vertices of the unshaded region are (4, 10), (4, 45) and (39, 10).

   The profit on x cows is R100x and the profit on y sheep is R50y.
   At (4, 10), the total profit = R [(4 × 100) + (10 × 50)] = R900.
   At (4, 45), the total profit = R [(4 × 100) + (45 × 50)] = R2600.
   At (39, 10), the total profit = R [(39 × 100) + (10 × 50)] = R4500.

   Hence, the maximum profit is R4500.

Example 2

A car dealer has two depots, A and B, and three showrooms, R, S and T. The distances in kilometres between the depots and the showrooms are shown in the table below.

	To		
	R	S	T
From A	3	4	2
From B	2	1	2

The dealer has 40 cars at depot A and 25 cars at depot B.
He receives orders from showrooms R, S and T for 20, 30 and 15 cars respectively.

How many cars should be sent from each depot to each showroom so that the total distance travelled by the cars is as little as possible?

Solution

Let the number of cars that travel from A to R be x
and the number of cars that travel from A to S be y.
20 cars are required at R so $(20 - x)$ cars must travel from B to R.
All 65 cars are required at the showrooms, so all 40 cars at A must be sent to the showrooms. It follows that $(40 - x - y)$ cars are sent from A to T. In this way, we can draw up a table for the number of cars going from each depot to each showroom.

	To		
	R	S	T
From A	x	y	$40 - x - y$
From B	$20 - x$	$30 - y$	$x + y - 25$

Each of the six numbers in this table must be a positive whole number or zero. It follows that $0 \leq x \leq 20$, $0 \leq y \leq 30$ and $25 \leq x + y \leq 40$.

The unshaded region in the diagram on the next page represents this set of inequalities.

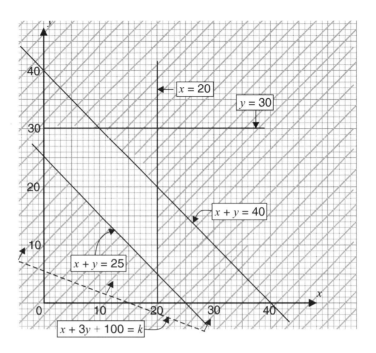

Using the distances between the depots and the showrooms:
Total distance (in kilometres) travelled by the cars
$= 3x + 4y + 2(40 - x - y) + 2(20 - x) + 1(30 - y) + 2(x + y - 25)$
$= 3x + 4y + 80 - 2x - 2y + 40 - 2x + 30 - y + 2x + 2y - 50$
$= x + 3y + 100$

We have to make this distance as small as possible, subject to the inequalities we have obtained.

Consider the line $x + 3y + 100 = k$. Moving this line parallel to itself, towards the top right of the diagram, the first point of contact with the unshaded region is (20, 5).

Hence, the smallest possible total distance $= (20 + 15 + 100)$ km $= 135$ km. This occurs when $x = 20$ and $y = 5$.

Alternative method The vertices of the region are (0, 25), (0, 30), (10, 30), (20, 20) and (20, 5). The values of $x + 3y + 100$ at these points are 175, 190, 200, 180 and 135. The smallest of these is 135 so the smallest possible distance $= 135$ km.

So, to answer the question, the smallest possible distance travelled occurs when $x = 20$ and $y = 5$. This means that:

20 cars must be sent from depot A to showroom R
5 cars must be sent from depot A to showroom S
15 cars must be sent from depot A to showroom T
25 cars must be sent from depot B to showroom S

Example 3

A firm manufactures two kinds of cotton cloth, 'Super' and 'Standard'. One metre of Super cloth needs 0.3kg of grey cotton, 0.4kg of red cotton and 0.1kg of blue cotton. One metre of Standard cloth needs 0.45kg of grey cotton, 0.2kg of red cotton and 0.1kg of blue cotton. The firm has 2250kg of grey cotton, 2000kg of red cotton and 600kg of blue cotton.

The profit on each metre of cloth is R3 for Super cloth and R2.50 for Standard cloth.

What is the maximum profit the firm can make on the cotton it has available?

Solution

Let the length of Super cloth made be x metres and the length of Standard cloth made be y metres.

Obviously, the firm cannot manufacture a negative length of cloth, and so $x \geq 0$ and $y \geq 0$.

The amount of grey cotton needed for x m of Super cloth and
y m of Standard cloth $= (0.3 \times x) + (0.45 \times y)$ kg
$= (0.3x + 0.45y)$ kg

2250kg of grey cotton is available so $0.3x + 0.45y \leq 2250$
$$30x + 45y \leq 225\,000$$

This inequality simplifies to $2x + 3y \leq 15\,000$

Similarly, considering the amount of red cotton available:
$$(0.4 \times x) + (0.2 \times y) \leq 2000$$
$$\text{That is } 4x + 2y \leq 20\,000$$
This inequality simplifies to $2x + y \leq 10\,000$

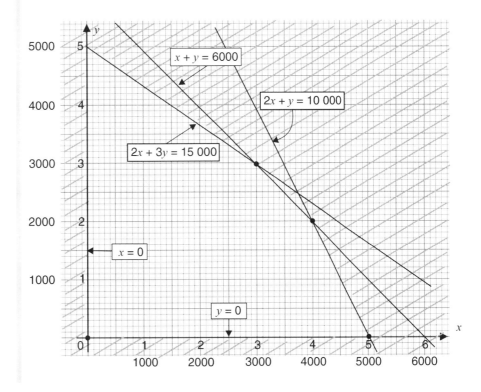

Considering the amount of blue cotton available:
$(0.1 \times x) + (0.1 \times y) \leq 600$
That is $x + y \leq 6000$

We now have five inequalities which must be satisfied simultaneously:

$x \geq 0, \ y \geq 0, \ 2x + 3y \leq 15\ 000, \ 2x + y \leq 10\ 000, \ x + y \leq 6000$

The unshaded region in the diagram represents this set of inequalities.

The total profit made on x m of Super cloth and y m of Standard cloth
$= R\ (3 \times x) + R\ (2.50 \times y)$
$= R\ (3x + 2.5y)$

The vertices of the unshaded region are
(0, 0), (0, 5000), (3000, 3000), (4000, 2000) and (5000, 0)
   At (0, 0) profit = R0
   At (0, 5000) profit = R (0 + 2.5 × 5000) = R12 500
   At (3000, 3000) profit = R (3 × 3000 + 2.5 × 3000) = R16 500
   At (4000, 2000) profit = R (3 × 4000 + 2.5 × 2000) = R17 000
   At (5000, 0) profit = R (3 × 5000 + 0) = R15 000

So the maximum profit that can be made is R17 000 (by making 4000m of Super cloth and 2000m of Standard cloth).

Summary

You started this unit with a section on functions:
- $f(x) = 2x + 3$, $y = 2x + 3$ and $f: x \mapsto 2x + 3$ are different ways of writing the same thing
- $gf(x)$ is a composite function – you find $f(x)$ first and then apply g to the answer you get
- you can use flow diagrams to help you find the inverse $f^{-1}(x)$ of the function $f(x)$ or you can change the subject of the formula to x and then replace y with x.

When drawing graphs of inequalities:
- use a solid line to show $\leq$ or $\geq$ and a dotted line to show $<$ or $>$
- check which region to shade using the x- and y-coordinates of a point
- shade the unwanted region – the solution is the unshaded region.

The last section introduced you to linear programming:
- write inequalities using the information and draw these on a graph
- the vertices of the unshaded region give the possible points giving the maximum or minimum results
- test for the maximum or minimum results by substituting the x- and y-coordinates of the vertices into the expression for maximum or minimum values.

This work has been quite challenging. Once you have mastered it work through the 'Check your progress' and then take a break before joining me to do geometry in Module 4.

You will find practical problems on linear programming in the 'Check your progress'. This exercise is the final one in Module 3 and is a revision exercise on all the material in Unit 4.

Check your progress

1. f and g are the functions $f: x \mapsto x - 5$ and $g: x \mapsto 5 - x$. Which of the following are true and which are false?
   a) $f^{-1} = g$
   b) $g^{-1}: x \mapsto 5 - x$
   c) $fg: x \mapsto -x$
   d) $fg = gf$

2. $f(x) = 3x^2 - 2x - 4$ and $g(x) = 4 - 3x$
   a) State the value of $f(-2)$.
   b) Solve the equation $f(x) = -3$.
   c) Solve the equation $f(x) = 0$, giving your answers correct to 2 decimal places.
   d) Solve the equation $g(x) = 2g(x) - 1$.
   e) Find $g^{-1}(x)$.

3. a) By shading the unwanted regions in the diagram below, show the region which satisfies all the inequalities
   $y \geq \frac{1}{2}x + 1$, $5x + 6y \leq 30$ and $y \leq x$.

   b) Given that x and y satisfy these three inequalities, find the greatest possible value of $x + 2y$.

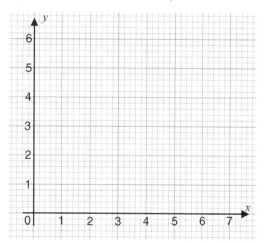

4. There are two popular electronic games, 'Cluedo' and 'Fantasy'. A retailer decides to order 60 Cluedo games and 40 Fantasy games.

   There are two suppliers, S and T.

   a) If the retailer orders x Cluedo games and y Fantasy games from S, how many of each type must he order from T? Write down the inequalities which express the fact that each of his orders must be a positive number or zero.

   b) The total number of games the retailer orders from S must not be more than 80. The total number he orders from T must not be more than 55. Write down two inequalities, in terms of x and y, which represent these restrictions.

c) On the graph paper supplied, show the region containing the points whose coordinates (x, y) satisfy all the inequalities you have obtained in parts a) and b).

shade the unwanted regions

d) Supplier S charges R90 for each Cluedo game and R180 for each Fantasy game. Supplier T charges R120 for each Cluedo game and R160 for each Fantasy game.
Show that the total cost of the retailer's order is R10 $(1360 - 3x + 2y)$, and find the values for x and y which make this cost as small as possible.

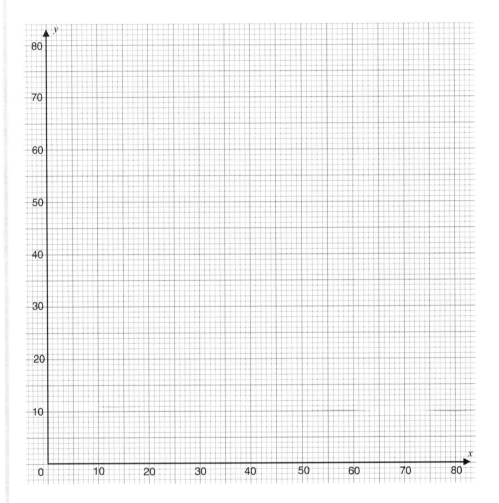

5. Arnie and Bernie are tailors. They make x jackets and y suits each week. Arnie does all the cutting and Bernie does all the sewing.

To make a jacket takes 5 hours of cutting and 4 hours of sewing. To make a suit takes 6 hours of cutting and 10 hours of sewing. Neither tailor works for more than 60 hours a week.

a) For the sewing, show that $2x + 5y \leq 30$.
b) Write down another inequality in x and y for the cutting.
c) They make at least 8 jackets a week. Write down another inequality.
d) (i) Draw axes from 0 to 16, using 1cm to represent 1 unit on each axis.
   (ii) On your grid, show the information in parts a), b), c). Shade the *unwanted* regions.
e) The profit on a jacket is R30 and on a suit is R100. Calculate the maximum profit that Arnie and Bernie can make in a week.

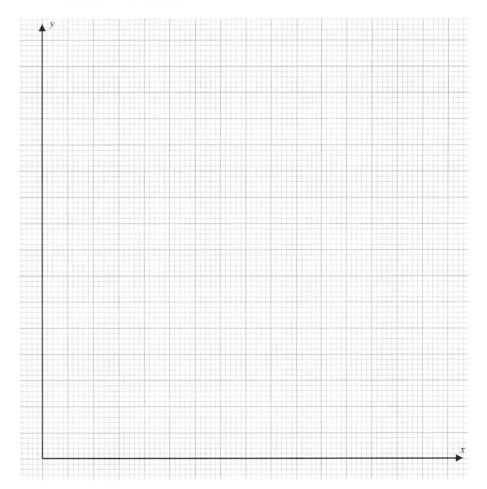

Check your answers at the end of this module.

Solutions

EXERCISE 1

1. a) P has coordinates (1, 3)
       Q has coordinates (−2, 2)
       R has coordinates (−1, −1)
       S has coordinates (2, 0)
    b) A square is formed. (Notice that this depends on the fact that the scale on the *x*-axis is the same as the scale on the *y*-axis.)

2. a)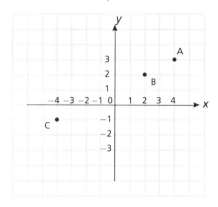

    b) The line crosses the *x*-axis at (−2, 0) and the *y*-axis at (0, 1).

3. a)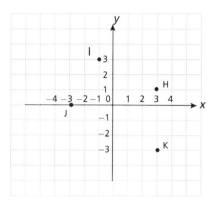

    b) The lines IH and JK are parallel.
    c) A trapezium is formed. (This is a quadrilateral with two sides parallel.)

EXERCISE 2

1. a) 0.1 year   b) R100
    c) R4700
    d) 3.5 years (or 3 years 6 months)
    e) 2 years (R4000 after 2.5 years and R6000 after 4.5 years)
    f) 3 years (this is where the graph is steepest)

2. a) 4 pounds   b) 2 kg
    c) 36 kg   d) 136 pounds
    e) (ii) should be 18 kg = 40 pounds or 18 pounds = 8 kg
       (iii) should be 60 pounds = 27 kg

3. a) (i) 2 years
       (ii) 100 million people
    b)

    c) (i) Any year from 1944 to 1950 would be regarded as correct provided it clearly comes from the graph you have drawn.
       (ii) Any number from 4.35 thousand million to 4.50 thousand million is accepted provided it clearly comes from the graph you have drawn.
       (iii) Any number from 50 million to 200 million.
       (iv) The world population is increasing and at an increasing rate.

4. a) 720 m   b) 7 minutes
    c) 0907 hours and 0921 hours
    d) Going to the supermarket. (She took 10 minutes to get to the supermarket but the return journey took 13 minutes.)

5. Each small square on the horizontal axis represents $\frac{1}{12}$ of an hour (5 minutes).

    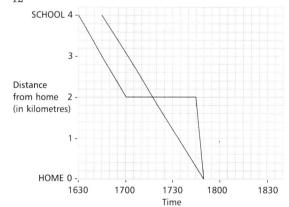

    a) 45 minutes (9 small squares)
    b) 1750 (4 small squares after 1730)
    c) (i) See graph   (ii) About 1717 or 1718.

EXERCISE 3

1. a) 1500 m
   b) speed = $\frac{\text{distance}}{\text{time}}$

   $= \frac{1200 \text{ m}}{10 \text{ minutes}}$

   $= \frac{120 \text{ m}}{\text{minute}}$

   $= \frac{120 \text{ m}}{60 \text{ s}}$

   $= 2$ m/s
   c) Ibrahim is stationary
   d) speed = $\frac{\text{distance}}{\text{time}}$

   $= \frac{600 \text{ m}}{20 \text{ minutes}}$

   $= \frac{30 \text{ m}}{\text{minute}}$

   $= \frac{30 \text{ m}}{60 \text{ s}}$

   $= 0.5$ m/s

2. a) 'The rate at which the car is slowing down' means the deceleration.
   This is $\frac{(10-4) \text{ m/s}}{3 \text{ s}} = 2$ m/s^2.
   b) Distance travelled = area under the speed–time graph = $\frac{1}{2}(6 \times 3) + (4 \times 3) + \frac{1}{2}(4 \times 7)$
   $= (9 + 12 + 14)$ m
   $= 35$ m
   c) Average speed = $\frac{\text{distance}}{\text{time}}$

   $= \frac{35 \text{ m}}{10 \text{ s}}$

   $= 3.5$ m/s

3. a) The speed increases from 0 to 20 m/s in 20 seconds.
   Acceleration = $\frac{20 \text{ m/s}}{20 \text{ s}} = 1$ m/s^2
   b) Distance travelled in last 10 seconds
   = area under graph from t = 50 to t = 60
   $= \frac{1}{2}(10 \times 20)$ m = 100 m
   c) Total distance travelled in 60 seconds
   = area under graph from t = 0 to t = 60
   $= \frac{1}{2}(20 \times 20) + (20 \times 30) + \frac{1}{2}(20 \times 10)$ m
   $= (200 + 600 + 100)$ m
   $= 900$ m
   Average speed = $\frac{900 \text{ m}}{60 \text{ s}}$
   $= 15$ m/s

Check your progress 1

1. a) P is (2, 1), Q is (0, 3), R is (−1, 1)
   b) The three possible positions of S are (3, 3), (−3, 3) and (1, −1).

2. a) R70 b) $2\frac{1}{2}$ hours
   c) $p = 35$ (where the graph meets the cost axis)
   $q = 20$ (for 1 hour, cost = R55 which is $p + 20$)

3. a) 4 °C b) 100 °C
   c) 14.5 minutes d) $\frac{180 \text{ °C}}{16 \text{ minutes}} = 11.25$ °C/minute
   e) Gas. Graph is steeper for the gas section than for any other section.

4. a) Graph is a straight line joining (0, 0) to (40, 152).
   b) 24 gallons c) $5 \times 3.8 = 19$ km

5. a)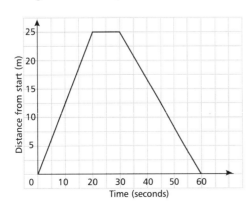
   b) 15m c) 5m

6. a) 1.5 km/minute = 1.5×60 km/h
   $= 90$ km/h
   b) $\frac{1.5 \text{ km/minute}}{5 \text{ minutes}} = 0.3$ km/minute^2
   c) Distance travelled = area under graph
   $= \frac{1}{2}(5 \times 1.5) + (5 \times 1.5) + \frac{1}{2}(5 \times 1.5)$
   $= (3.75 + 7.5 + 3.75)$ km
   $= 15$ km
   d) 3 minutes
   e) 0.25 km/minute or 15 km/h
   f) Distance travelled between 18 minutes and 25 minutes = area under graph
   $= \frac{1}{2}(2 \times 0.5) + (3 \times 0.5) + \frac{1}{2}(2 \times 0.5)$
   $= 0.5 + 1.5 + 0.5$
   $= 2.5$ km
   Distance between stations $= (15 + 2.5)$ km
   $= 17.5$ km

EXERCISE 4

1.
x	-2	0	2	4	6
y	-2	-1	0	1	2

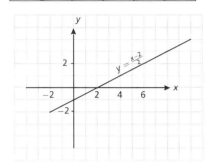

2.
x	-2	-1	0	1	2	3	4
y	11	8	5	2	-1	-4	-7

The line crosses the x-axis at the point (1.7, 0).

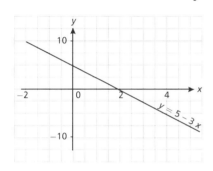

3. The graphs intersect at the point (2.5, 1.5).

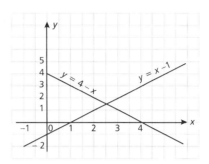

4. The graphs are parallel straight lines.

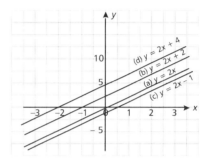

EXERCISE 5

1. I substituted $x = 0$ to find $y = 4$. So (0, 4) is on the line. Then I substituted $y = 0$ to find $x = 5$. So (5, 0) is also on the line.
Re-arranging $4x + 5y = 20$
gives $5y = -4x + 20$
and so $y = -\frac{4}{5}x + 4$

Hence, gradient $= -\frac{4}{5}$

This can also be obtained from the graph by taking, for example, the points (0, 4) and (5, 0).

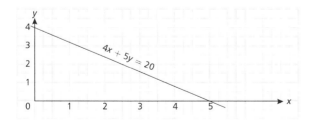

2. a) $4y = 3x - 24$ so $y = \frac{3}{4}x - 6$ and gradient $= \frac{3}{4}$.

b) $5y = -4x - 6$ so $y = -\frac{4}{5}x - \frac{6}{5}$ and gradient $= -\frac{4}{5}$.

c) $2y = x - 3$ so $y = \frac{1}{2}x - \frac{3}{2}$ and gradient $= \frac{1}{2}$.

3. The first line is $y = \frac{1}{2}x - \frac{3}{4}$ so has gradient $\frac{1}{2}$.

The second line is $y = \frac{1}{2}x - \frac{5}{6}$ so has gradient $\frac{1}{2}$.

The lines have the same gradient so they are parallel.

4. Gradient PQ $= \frac{-1-4}{2-0} = -\frac{5}{2}$

5. Take (for example) the points (2, 0) and (4, 3) which are on the line.
Gradient $= \frac{3-0}{4-2} = \frac{3}{2}$

EXERCISE 6

1. a) Gradient = −3, intercept on y-axis = 4.
    b) The line is $y = \frac{1}{2}x + 2$ so gradient $= \frac{1}{2}$ and intercept on y-axis = 2.
    c) The line is $y = -x + 3$ so gradient $= -1$ and intercept on y-axis = 3.

2. a) $y = \frac{3}{5}x - 2$ which can be written as $5y = 3x - 10$.
    b) $y = -\frac{1}{2}x + \frac{3}{4}$ which can be written as $4y = -2x + 3$ or $2x + 4y = 3$.

3. a) Gradient = 1 and y-intercept = 2. Equation of line is $y = x + 2$.
    b) Gradient = 2 and y-intercept = −2. Equation of line is $y = 2x - 2$.
    c) Gradient = −1 and y-intercept = 3. Equation of line is $y = -x + 3$ which can be written as $x + y = 3$.

4. Gradient $= \frac{8-2}{7-5} = \frac{6}{2} = 3$ so equation of line is $y = 3x + c$.
    P(5, 2) is on the line so $2 = 15 + c$ and $c = -13$.
    The equation of the line is $y = 3x - 13$.

EXERCISE 7

1. $(EF)^2 = 8^2 + 15^2 = 64 + 225 = 289$
    Hence $EF = \sqrt{289} = 17$

2. $(AB)^2 = 9^2 + 12^2 = 81 + 144 = 225$
    Hence $AB = \sqrt{225} = 15$

3. $(CD)^2 = 10^2 + 24^2 = 100 + 576 = 676$
    Hence $CD = \sqrt{676} = 26$

4. $(GH)^2 = 6^2 + 9^2 = 36 + 81 = 117$
    Hence $GH = \sqrt{117} = 10.8$ (to 3 s.f.)

EXERCISE 8

1.

x	−4	−3	−2	−1	0	1	2
x^2	16	9	4	1	0	1	4
$+2x$	−8	−6	−4	−2	0	+2	+4
y	8	3	0	−1	0	3	8

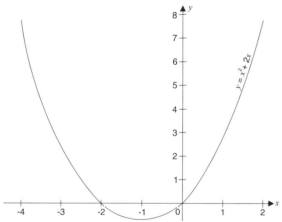

2.

x	−2	−1	0	1	2	3	4	5	6	7
x^2	4	1	0	1	4	9	16	25	36	49
$-5x$	+10	+5	0	−5	−10	−15	−20	−25	−30	−35
-4	−4	−4	−4	−4	−4	−4	−4	−4	−4	−4
y	10	2	−4	−8	−10	−10	−8	−4	2	10

The lowest point on the graph is (2.5, −10.25).

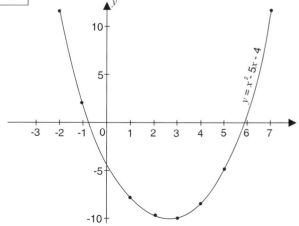

EXERCISE 8 (cont.)

3.

x	-3	-2	-1	0	1	2	3
y	-5	0	3	4	3	0	-5

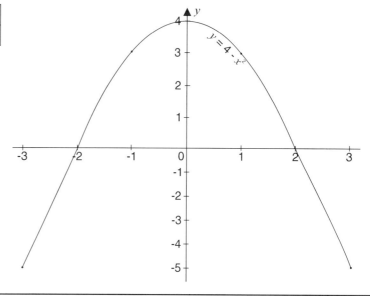

EXERCISE 9

1.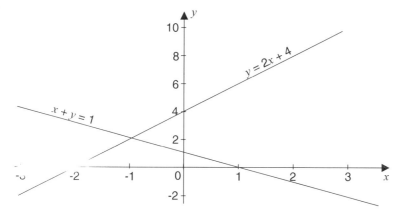

The solution is $x = -1$, $y = 2$.

2.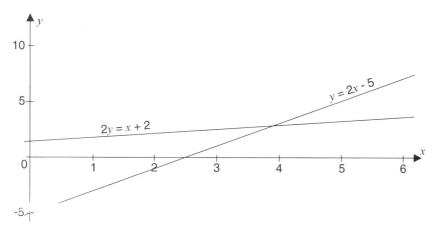

The solution is $x = 4$, $y = 3$.

3. a) The lines cross at the point $(3, 2)$ so the solution of the simultaneous equations $2x + 3y = 12$, $x - y = 1$ is $x = 3$, $y = 2$.
    Check: When $x = 3$ and $y = 2$, $2x + 3y = 6 + 6 = 12$ ✓
    and $x - y = 3 - 2 = 1$ ✓ } The solution is checked.

    b) The lines cross at the point $(-1, 2)$ so the solution of the simultaneous equations $y = 2x + 4$, $x + y = 1$ is $x = -1$, $y = 2$.
    Check: When $x = -1$ and $y = 2$, $2x + 4 = -2 + 4 = 2 = y$ ✓
    and $x + y = -1 + 2 = 1$ ✓ } The solution is checked.

EXERCISE 10

1. a) The solutions are $x = -1$ and $x = 2$.
   b) The solutions are $x = -2.4$ and $x = 3.4$.
   c) The equation is equivalent to $x^2 - x - 2 = 4$, so the solutions are $x = -2$ and $x = 3$.

2. a) speed $= \frac{\text{distance}}{\text{time}}$

   so time $(y) = \frac{\text{distance}}{\text{speed }(x)} = \frac{240}{x}$

x	20	40	60	80	100	120
y	12	6	4	3	2.4	2

   b)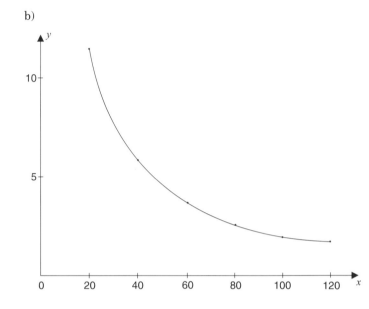

   c) $y = \frac{240}{x}$

Check your progress 2

1. a) (i) See graph

   (ii) Gradient $= 1$

   b) (i)
x	-6	-3	0	3
y	0	1	2	3

   (ii) See graph

   c) The graphs meet at $(-3, 1)$.

2. a) When $x = -2$, $y = 7$ and when $x = 0.5$, $y = 3.25$

   b)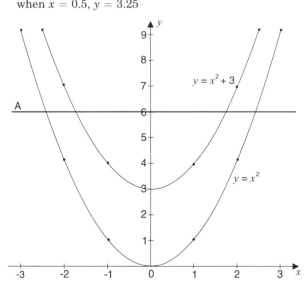

   c) No. For every value of x, the graph of $y = x^2 + 3$ is 3 units above the graph of $y = x^2$.

   d) (i) I used line A to find the solutions. The solutions are $x = 2.45$ and $x = -2.45$. (Answers between 2.4 and 2.5 numerically are acceptable.)
   (ii) The solutions are $x = 1.73$ and $x = -1.73$. (Answers between 1.7 and 1.8 numerically are acceptable.)

Check your progress 2 (cont.)

3. a) Method 1: Choose 2 points on the line and use
   gradient = $\frac{\text{increase in } y\text{-coordinate}}{\text{increase in } x\text{-coordinate}}$
   Taking the points $(-6, 6)$ and $(6, 0)$
   gradient = $\frac{0-6}{6-(-6)} = \frac{-6}{12} = -\frac{1}{2}$

   Method 2: Rearrange $x + 2y = 6$ to $2y = 6 - 2x$
   and then $y = 3 - \frac{1}{2}x$
   Gradient = coefficient of x when equation is in form $y = mx + c = -\frac{1}{2}$

   b) (i)

x	0	2	4
y	-3	0	3

   (ii) See graph

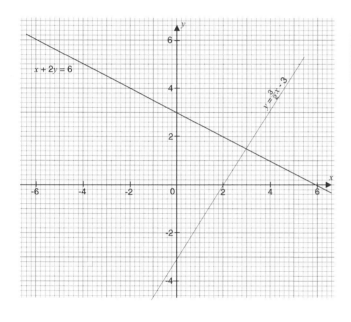

   c) Method 1: On the graph, the lines intersect at the point $(3, 1.5)$.
   The solution of the simultaneous equations is $x = 3$, $y = 1.5$.

   Method 2: Since the question does not say that the graph must be used, we can use the method of substitution.
   From $x + 2y = 6$ we obtain $x = 6 - 2y$.
   Substituting in $y = \frac{3}{2}x - 3$ we obtain
   $y = \frac{3}{2}(6 - 2y) - 3$.
   Hence, $y = 9 - 3y - 3$ and so $4y = 6$ and $y = 1.5$.
   Substituting in $x = 6 - 2y$ we deduce that $x = 3$.
   So the solution is $x = 3$, $y = 1.5$.

4. a) $(CS)^2 = (11 - 7)^2 + (4 - 1)^2$
   $= 16 + 9$
   $= 25$
   so $CS = \sqrt{25} = 5$

   b) Greatest distance = CS + radius of circle
   $= 5 + 3$
   $= 8$

EXERCISE 11

1. a)

x	0	1	2	3	4
y	0	3	0	-3	0

   c) (i) $x = 0, 2, 4$ (ii) $x = 0.7, 1, 4.3$

   b)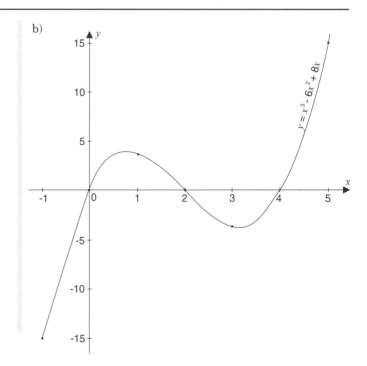

EXERCISE 11 (cont.)

2. Solutions of the equation $x^3 - 3x^2 = 3x - 2$ are the x-coordinates of the points where the graphs of $y = x^3 - 3x^2$ and $y = 3x - 2$ cross.

   From the diagram, these are
   $x = -1.1$,
   $x = 0.45$
   and $x = 3.65$

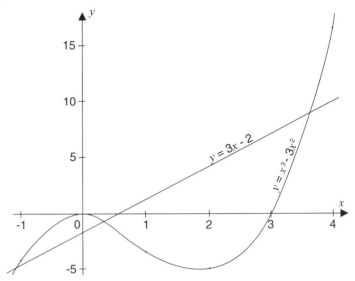

EXERCISE 12

1. a)

x	1	1.5	2	2.5	3	3.5	4	4.5	5
y	-9	-3.5	0	2.7	5	7.1	9	10.8	12.6

   b)

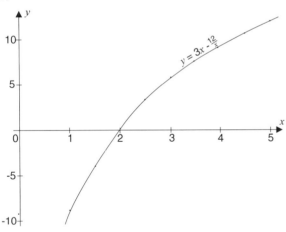

2. a) (i) 2 (ii) 0.8
   b) Line to be drawn is $y = 8 - 5x$.
      Solution of $10^x = 8 - 5x$ is $x = 0.67$.

   c) (i) $x = 4.27$ (values from 4.2 to 4.3 acceptable)
      (ii) $x = 1.33$ (values from 1.3 to 1.4 acceptable)

EXERCISE 13

1. a) (i) 4 (ii) -2
   b) Using the symmetry of the curve about the y-axis, the point required is $(-1.5, 2.25)$.

2. The gradient is -5.
   The gradient represents the rate at which the population is changing. In this particular case, in 1950, the population of the village was decreasing by 5 per year.

Check your progress 3

1. a) $p = -10.0, q = 6.3, r = 9.2$

    b)

    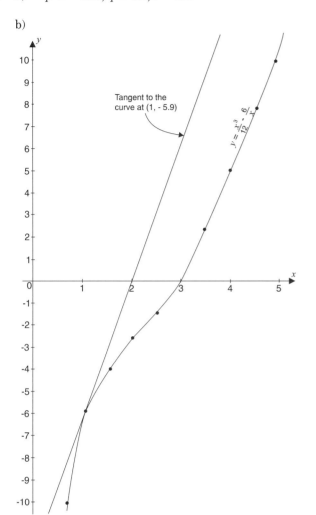

    c) $x = 2.9$
    d) Gradient = 6.25 (values from 5.75 to 6.75 acceptable).

2. a) VI
    b) II
    c) I
    d) IV

3. a) (i) $p = 160 \times 2^0 = 160 \times 1 = 160$

        $q = 160 \times 2^{-4} = 160 \times \frac{1}{16} = 10$

        $r = 160 \times 2^{-6} = 160 \times \frac{1}{64} = 2.5$

        (Note: In the table of values, each value of M is half the previous one.)

        (ii) See the graph below.

        (iii) The tangent at the point (2, 40) has been drawn. Taking the points (0, 95) and (3.4, 0) on this tangent,
        gradient $= \frac{0 - 95}{3.4 - 0} = -27.9$

        When $t = 2$, the rate of change of mass $= -27.9$ grams per minute. (Answers from -25 to -35 grams per minute are acceptable.)

    b) Since $m = 160 - M$, the two chemicals have equal mass when $m = M = 80$.
        From the graph (or the table of values), $M = 80$ when $t = 1$.

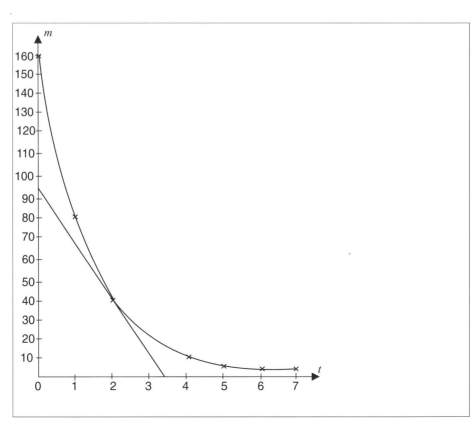

EXERCISE 14

1. a) $f(2) = 8 - 8 = 0$
   b) $f(-1) = -1 - 8 = -9$
   c) $g(5) = 3 - 5 = -2$
   d) $g(-2) = 3 - (-2) = 3 + 2 = 5$

2. a) $4 \times 4 = 16$
   b) $4 \times 4 = 16$
   c) $4 \times \frac{1}{4} = 1$

3. a) $x^2 - x = 6$ so $x^2 - x - 6 = 0$ which factorised is $(x - 3)(x + 2) = 0$. The solutions are $x = 3$ and $x = -2$.
   b) $x^2 - x = x^2 + 3x - 12$ simplifies to $12 = 4x$. The solution is $x = 3$.

4. a) $f(\frac{1}{2}) = \frac{4\frac{1}{2}}{\frac{1}{2}} = 9$
   b) $\frac{4+x}{x} = 3$ simplifies to $4 + x = 3x$, and then to $4 = 2x$. The solution is $x = 2$.

EXERCISE 15

a) $g[h(1)] = g[5] = 25 + 1 = 26$
b) $h[g(1)] = h[2] = 4 + 3 = 7$
c) $g[g(2)] = g[5] = 25 + 1 = 26$
d) $h[h(5)] = h[13] = 26 + 3 = 29$

EXERCISE 16

1. $f^{-1}(x) = \frac{x-3}{4}$

2. $g^{-1}(x) = 3(x + 4)$ or $g^{-1}(x) = 3x + 12$

3. $h^{-1}(x) = \frac{x}{2} + 3$
   a) $h^{-1}(10) = 8$
   b) $h[h^{-1}(20)] = h[13] = 20$
   c) $h^{-1}[h^{-1}(26)] = h^{-1}[16] = 8 + 3 = 11$

EXERCISE 17

1.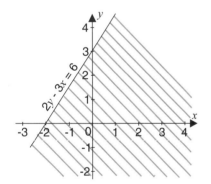

2.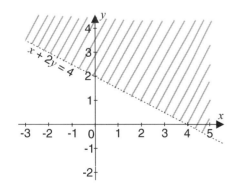

3.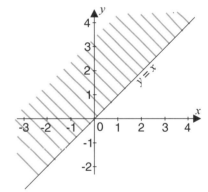

4. a) $y \geq 3x + 3$
   b) $x + y < 3$

EXERCISE 18

1.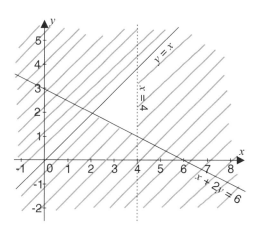

2.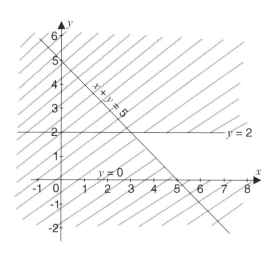

3.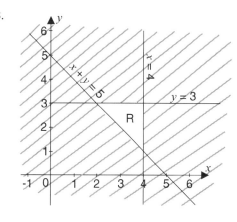

4. $y > 2x + 1, x + y \leq 4, x \leq 2$

5. $(-1, 4)$, $(0, 2)$, $(0, 3)$, $(1, 0)$, $(1, 1)$, $(1, 2)$, $(2, 0)$, $(2, 1)$, $(3, 0)$

EXERCISE 19

1. Calculate the values of $3x + 2y$ at the vertices of the unshaded region.
   At $(-2, 6)$, $3x + 2y = -6 + 12 = 6$.
   At $(4, 0)$, $3x + 2y = 12 + 0 = 12$.
   At $(6, 0)$, $3x + 2y = 18 + 0 = 18$.
   At $(6, 6)$, $3x + 2y = 18 + 12 = 30$.

   Greatest possible value of $3x + 2y$ is 30 and least possible value is 6.

   You may also have drawn a line with gradient $-\frac{3}{2}$ to find the correct points to substitute for the greatest and least possible values.

2. a)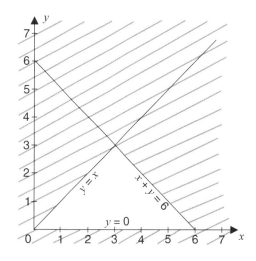

   b) At $(0, 0)$, $2x + y = 0$.
      At $(6, 0)$, $2x + y = 12$.
      At $(3, 3)$, $2x + y = 9$.
      Hence, greatest possible value of $2x + y$ is 12.

EXERCISE 19 (cont.)

3.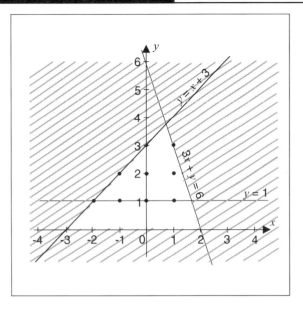

The points (x, y) marked in the diagram satisfy the three given inequalities (taking into account that x and y are whole numbers).

Consider the line $x + y = k$ moving from bottom left to top right. The first point of contact is $(-2, 1)$ where $x + y = -1$. The last point of contact is $(1, 3)$ where $x + y = 4$.

Hence, the greatest and least possible values of $x + y$ are 4 and -1 respectively.

Check your progress 4

1. a) $f^{-1} : x \mapsto x + 5$ so the statement $f^{-1} = g$ is *false*.
   b) Let $g(x) = y$. That is $y = 5 - x$ which gives $x = 5 - y$.
   g^{-1} maps y onto x so $g^{-1}(y) = 5 - y$.
   Hence, changing the 'dummy variable',
   $g^{-1}(x) = 5 - x$.
   The statement $g^{-1} : x \mapsto 5 - x$ is *true*.
   c) $f[g(x)] = f[5 - x] = (5 - x) - 5 = -x$.
   The statement $fg : x \mapsto -x$ is *true*.
   d) $g[f(x)] = g[x - 5] = 5 - (x - 5)$
   $= 5 - x + 5$
   $= 10 - x$.
   The statement $fg = gf$ is *false*.

2. a) $f(-2) = 3(4) - 2(-2) - 4 = 12 + 4 - 4 = 12$
   b) Rearranging $3x^2 - 2x - 4 = -3$ gives
   $3x^2 - 2x - 1 = 0$.
   Hence, $(x - 1)(3x + 1) = 0$.
   The solutions of $f(x) = -3$ are $x = 1$ and $x = -\frac{1}{3}$.
   c) Using the quadratic equation formula, the solutions of $3x^2 - 2x - 4 = 0$ are
   $x = \frac{2 \pm \sqrt{4 + 48}}{6} = \frac{2 \pm 7.211}{6}$
   $= 1.5351$ or -0.8685
   The solution of $f(x) = 0$ are $x = 1.54$ and $x = -0.87$ to 2 dec. places.
   d) $g(x) = 2g(x) - 1$ simplifies to $g(x) = 1$ and so $4 - 3x = 1$.
   The solution of the equation is $x = 1$.
   e) Let g map x onto y. That is $y = 4 - 3x$.
   Hence $x = \frac{4 - y}{3}$.
   g^{-1} maps y onto x so $g^{-1}(y) = \frac{4 - y}{3}$.
   Changing the 'dummy variable' to x, we get
   $g^{-1}(x) = \frac{4 - x}{3}$.

3. a)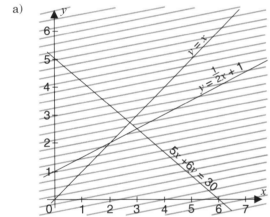

   b) The vertices of the unshaded region are $(2, 2)$, $(3, 2.5)$ and $(2.7, 2.7)$.
   At $(2, 2)$, $x + 2y = 6$.
   At $(3, 2.5)$, $x + 2y = 8$.
   At $(2.7, 2.7)$, $x + 2y = 8.1$
   The greatest possible value of $x + 2y$ is 8.1

4. a) He must order $(60 - x)$ Cluedo games and $(40 - y)$ Fantasy games from T.
   $0 \leq x \leq 60$ and $0 \leq y \leq 40$.
   b) $x + y \leq 80$ and $(60 - x) + (40 - y) \leq 55$ so $45 \leq x + y \leq 80$.

Check your progress 4 (cont.)

c)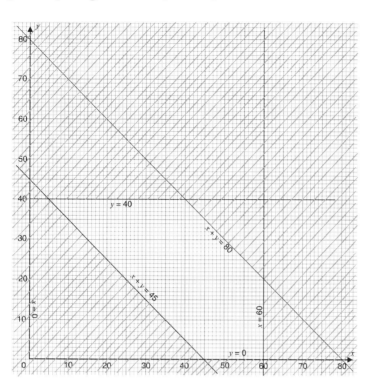

d) Total cost = R[90x + 180y + 120(60 − x) + 160(40 − y)]
   = R[90x + 180y + 7200 − 120x + 6400 − 160y]
   = R[13 600 − 30x + 20y]
   = R10[1360 − 3x + 2y]

At (5, 40), total cost = R14 250.
At (45, 0), total cost = R12 250.
At (60, 0), total cost = R11 800
At (5, 40), total cost = R14 50.
At (60, 20), total cost = R12 200.
At (40, 40), total cost = R13 200.

Hence, the smallest possible cost = R11 800, when $x = 60$ and $y = 0$.

5. a) Time required for sewing = $(4x + 10y)$ hours. Bernie does all the sewing, so this time must not be more than 60 hours. Hence, $4x + 10y \leq 60$ which simplifies to $2x + 5y \leq 30$.
   b) Time required for cutting = $(5x + 6y)$ hours. It follows that $5x + 6y \leq 60$.
   c) $x \geq 8$
   d) The boundaries of the required region are $2x + 5y = 30$, $5x + 6y = 60$ and $x = 8$. The unwanted regions are shaded on the graph paper.
   e) x and y must be whole numbers. The relevant grid points have been marked on the graph paper. The weekly profit = $R(30x + 100y)$. Considering the moving line $30x + 100y = k$, or working out the profit at each relevant grid point, we find that the maximum profit occurs when $x = 9$ and $y = 2$. The maximum profit = R(270 + 200) = R470.

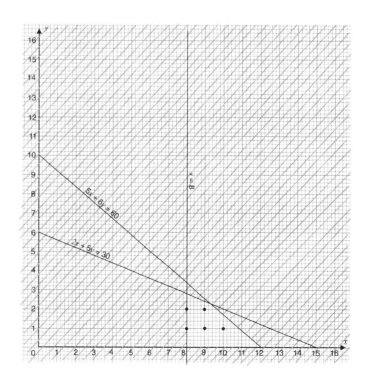

Index

A
accelerating 19
axis
    x- 2
    y- 2

C
cartesian geometry 1
changing subject of
   formula 34
composite functions 86
conversion graphs 8
coordinate 1
coordinate geometry 1
cubic functions 63

D
decelerating 19
distance-time graphs 10

E
equations
    linear simultaneous 34
exponential function 69

F
flow diagrams 87
formula
    changing subject of 34
function(s) 44, 83
    composite 86
    cubic 63
    exponential 69
    growth 69
    inverse of a 87
    quadratic 44
    reciprocal 50

G
geometry
    cartesian 1
    coordinate 1
gradient 16
    of a straight line 35
graphs
    conversion 8
    distance-time 10
    speed-time 19
    straight line 29
    travel 10
growth function 69

H
hyperbola
    rectangular 50

I
inequality 90
    simultaneous 95
intercept
    y- 39
inverse of a function 87

L
linear
    programming 99
    simultaneous equations 34
lines
    parallel 36

O
ordered pair 2
origin 2

P
pair
    ordered 2
parabola 45
parallel lines 36
programming
    linear 99
Pythagoras's theorem 42

Q
quadratic functions 44

R
reciprocal functions 50
rectangular hyperbola 50

S
simultaneous inequalities 95
speed-time graphs 19
straight line graphs 29

T
tangent 75
travel graphs 10

V
velocity 17

X
x-axis 2

Y
y-axis 2
y-intercept 39